# God Be In My Mouth

# God Be In My Mouth

*40 ways to grow as a preacher*

Doug Gay

SAINT ANDREW PRESS
Edinburgh

First published in 2018 by
SAINT ANDREW PRESS
121 George Street
Edinburgh EH2 4YN

Copyright © Doug Gay 2018

ISBN 978-0-86153-996-3

Scripture quotations are from the New Revised Standard Version of the Bible, Anglicized Edition, copyright © 1989, 1995 by the Division of Christian Education of the National Council of the Churches of Christ in the USA. Used by permission. All rights reserved.

The author and publisher acknowledge use of copyright material from T. S. Eliot, 'Choruses from "The Rock" IX', in Collected Poems 1909–1962, Faber & Faber, 1963. Permission sought.

British Library Cataloguing in Publication Data

A catalogue record for this book is available from the British Library.

It is the publisher's policy to only use papers that are natural and recyclable and that have been manufactured from timber grown in renewable, properly managed forests. All of the manufacturing processes of the papers are expected to conform to the environmental regulations of the country of origin.

Typeset by Regent Typesetting
Printed and bound in the United Kingdom by
CPI Group (UK) Ltd, Croydon

# Contents

## Part 3  Speaking

## Part 4  Living

*With gratitude,*
*to those (some without knowing it or me)*
*who taught and still teach me to preach*

Eric Alexander
John Stott
Donald Macleod
Lance Stone
Gordon Palmer
Malcolm Cuthbertson
John Bell
David Jasper
Stephen D. Moore
Leith Fisher
Sam Wells
Thomas Long
Chris Boesel
Heather Walton
Stuart Blythe
Allan Rudy-Froese
Anna Carter Florence
Nadia Bolz Weber
Padraig ÓTuama

# Introduction

I have hesitated about writing this book, both because I think preaching is a hard thing to 'teach' and because I am very aware how much I myself still have to learn.

Specialists in homiletics – the study of preaching – are more common in North America than they are in the UK, where they have become an endangered species. Although I teach across the practical theology curriculum, I have been teaching preaching in various forms to ministry students (and a few other interested parties) at Glasgow University for the last ten years. This book represents the fruits of my reflection on that period and my thoughts on what has helped me in my own practice. The subtitle is meant as testimony to what has helped me to grow as a preacher.

My own reading in homiletics has left me gently sceptical about over-elaborated treatments of homiletic method. I applaud those who have the stamina to make such contributions, but I have not always found them interesting to read or helpful in practice. When I began to work in the field of practical theology, scholars such as Don Browning were moving the discipline on from the view that it was mainly about 'hints and tips' for working pastors. I understand why that was right and necessary, but I think that within practical theology different areas of practice call for different approaches.

Along with the teaching of drama, the closest model for 'teaching preaching' in a university or seminary setting may be the teaching of creative writing. Histories of poetry, the novel or the short story show how patterns of genre and form can converge and stabilise, sometimes for very long periods of time. They also demonstrate how they can be taken up in different ways by different voices, how they can be subverted and hybridised by those using them, and how innovation often takes the form of creative transgression of the existing 'rules'. We are helped here by Alasdair MacIntyre's definition of tradition as an argument extended through time about the nature of the good. Or we could think of Stanley Hauerwas's elaborations on that in relation to the nature of a craft: his favourite example is, famously, bricklaying.

For those doing the teaching, then, the trick is to encourage students to learn through reflecting on previous practice, helping them to understand the tradition they stand in, while still expecting and enabling them to be creative in their own preaching. That means caution about introducing homiletic methods that are too prescriptive, but it also means sound judgement about what counts as effective innovation or experimentation.

In this book I have brought together brief reflections on learning to preach. It is a personal selection, based on what I (and I hope my students) have found helpful. By its very nature, it reflects dependence on the ideas and influences of others and I have tried to ensure all debts are acknowledged and attributed.

I have arranged these 40 reflections in four parts, so there is some logic to the order in which they are presented; but the book is also something I hope people will feel free to dip into when they are looking for a reminder or a stimulus for their own practice. In 1975, Brian Eno and Peter Schmidt first developed their *Oblique Strategies* resource, a set of cards that could be randomly drawn from by artists/musicians/thinkers who were experiencing a block or lack in their own thinking or practice.[1] This book is not that for preachers (although now I think of it, 'oblique preaching strategies' would be an interesting project), but it may be that it could be used in a similar way. Preachers or students of preaching can take it off the shelf and read a couple of entries almost randomly, when they are looking for some provocation, stimulus or encouragement. I say that because it is how many of these ideas work for me. On any given Sunday, for any given text, one or more of these ideas will be to the fore in my own mind, shaping how I develop and prepare a sermon.

This is not a comprehensive primer for preaching. There is much more to be said about how to structure sermons, about the use of examples and illustrations, about storytelling, delivery, etc. It circles around its subject, sometimes returning to the same topics and themes from what I hope is a new angle. I am a white, male Scottish Presbyterian, and therefore the book reflects the limits of my culture, context and experience – as well as the ways my identity blindsides me.

Preaching is a demanding privilege. It requires, but does not depend on, the best of our skill and creativity. It also requires more integrity, wisdom and love than most of us have to bring to it. My own experience of preaching over the past three decades has always been that I am troubled and haunted by a sense of my own inadequacies, but also that I have felt called to this ministry within the Church. I hope these reflections may be helpful to others who are also called to preaching.

The title of this book comes from a line in a famous sixteenth-century prayer, which I often pray either privately or publicly before preaching:

---

[1] See www.enoshop.co.uk/product/oblique-strategies.html for the latest edition.

God be in my head and in my understanding.
God be in my mine eyes and in my looking.
**God be in my mouth and in my speaking.**
God be in my heart and in my thinking,
God be at mine end and at my departing.

*Sarum Primer 1527*

*Doug Gay*
*Glasgow 2017*

# PART 1

# Preaching

# 1.1 Finding the year

I begin with the question of what to preach, and when.

I remember times in my own ministry, especially in the early years, when the prospect of preaching weighed heavily on me. The Sundays stretching ahead seemed like an endless series of demands, or even question marks about whether I could deliver. How would I ever find enough things to say? Looking back, one of the things that helped me to become a preacher and to sustain a preaching ministry was what I would call 'finding the year'. By that I mean three things.

## The liturgical year

The first is (and here all of my Roman Catholic, Lutheran and Episcopalian/Anglican friends and readers will have to yawn and bear with me) that over time I have become a more catholic kind of Presbyterian. In particular, I have come to trust the shape of the Christian Year, of the liturgical year. I have come to feel that it is somehow holding me and carrying me and moving me on. When I first shared that thought at a training day for preachers, I was surprised by how emotional it made me feel to express it. Without being too fanciful about it, there has been a sense that underneath these seasons, these long-established rhythms, were the everlasting arms. Through the shapes of these traditions, I have come to believe I am being sustained by God. That has affected my own spirituality very deeply, and I think it has also affected the spirituality of all the congregations and Christian communities I have been a part of. With every year that goes by, it means more to me that I live it through the rhythms of Advent, Christmas, Epiphany, Lent, Holy Week, Easter and Pentecost. The Canadian philosopher Charles Taylor characterises us as too often living in the flat, homogenous time of secular modernity. But as a preacher it has been true more and more with each passing year that I have not only been inhabiting that featureless landscape. In learning to live by the Christian Year, I have also been learning to live by a different time signature; I have been walking the contours of a different landscape, with its own dark valleys and sunlit heights.

I grew up in the Exclusive wing of the Darbyite Plymouth Brethren, where the liturgical year was scrupulously ignored, so that every Sunday was both Christmas and Easter. For the curious, that feels more or less exactly the same as no Sunday ever being Christmas or Easter. Not all of me has climbed up the candle,[1] but my timekeeping has. It matters to me as a preacher where I am in the Christian Year: whether I am preaching in Lent or at Pentecost. Each November, as I get ready for the start of Advent, there is a renewed sense of both anticipation and relief. Within this work of preaching, I believe that I, along with the whole worshipping community, am being held and shaped by something bigger and deeper, something older and richer than my own understanding.

## The lectionary year

If that was one way of finding the year, the lectionary has given me another one. I am not starry-eyed about the lectionary,[2] I recognise its faults and limitations but, in my case, finding

---

1 Or moved to a more 'high church' vision of liturgy.
2 I use the Revised Common Lectionary.

the shape of the lectionary helped to settle me as a preacher. The lectionary gave me an A and a B and a C – but it gave me them one at a time. What that did was to change my relationship with Scripture. I still get most stressed about preaching when for some reason I have to choose, from scratch, which passages to preach on. When I am working with the lectionary (and I think this can also be true of preachers who work with a non-lectionary-based expository series) somehow I relax. I have a sense of being given something to work with, of something to push back against, of something to wrestle with and something to receive. I sometimes describe this to students as the Texas Hold-Em homiletic, where you have to play the hand you are dealt. I am also reminded week by week of the variety of literary forms that Scripture comes in, as every Sunday I am exposed to at least three.

Since each year of the lectionary features one of the synoptic Gospels, that becomes a key feature of my year as a preacher: this is going to be the year of Luke ... but that is also true for the Old Testament and Epistles – this will be the year of Jeremiah, or Job or Galatians. I find myself looking ahead at the year with a sense of expectancy, as if I am waiting for a reunion with some old and very dear friends, who I haven't seen for too long. Things have not stood still since the last time we met. We have things to tell one another. Already in November, I know it is out of these coming conversations that this year's sermons will be born.

## The life year

The third way of finding the year has come through the growing understanding that I have to preach as myself. Every year I remind myself and my students about Ugandan Bishop Festo Kivengere's wise comment that when you preach you can't be like Jacob, pretending to be someone else in order to get the blessing. You have to preach out of your own life, you have to speak with your own voice, you have to be present with your own body. Preaching always takes place within a life year: the year I got married, the year I moved to London, the year my first child was born, the year Rachel's mum got sick, the year my dad died, the year Mandela was released, the year the Scottish Parliament was reconvened, the year I was twenty-six, the year I turned forty.

With the life year, like the lectionary, there is the sense of being given something to work with. Sometimes we are given something that feels unbearable, sometimes something that feels exhilarating. There is give and take, as the popular worship song by the Redmans puts it: 'you give and take away/you give and take away'. In the midst of that, there is the call to preach honestly. If we try to fake it, it will break us. The Christian activist Jim Wallis once wrote that 'we have nothing more to share with the world than we have ourselves'. In one sense, that means we have all the riches of the gospel to share, because all things are ours in Christ. But it's also true that if we try to live beyond our means emotionally, psychologically or existentially, that attempt will hollow us out. Along with our selves, our preaching voices will become hollow.

The life year is not just an individual thing; it is personal and local, but it is also political and global. It is what positions homiletics as 'contextual theology'. The life year will always find us, and find us out; but we also need to try to find it. This is one we are never done with: the struggle to preach in our own voice, in our own skin, in our own life, in our own place and time.

## Finding the year

What to preach, when? For me it involves finding the year: the liturgical year, the lectionary year, the life year. The key point here is, of course, that in our preaching these will all become one. They will become *this* year.

The next whole year that lies ahead as I finish this book, 2017–18, will contain all of the traditional seasons, fasts and feasts of the liturgical year. It will once again, for the eighth time in my life as a preacher, be Year B in the Revised Common Lectionary – the year of Mark, the year of 1 and 2 Corinthians, the year of Jonah, Deuteronomy, 1 and 2 Samuel. Some of the experiences it will hold for me and for the congregation I am part of, I can predict with some certainty; but many I cannot. It is also sobering to reflect that of course I cannot ever know whether I will be around for all or any of it. If I do live and preach through it, what is certain is that what happens within me and around me, what happens in my local neighbourhood and in the wider world, what happens in my life year, will have a crucial influence on my preaching.

Whenever I approach a new liturgical year, getting ready to begin again on Advent Sunday, I feel a great sense of anticipation and expectation. Whether or not we work with the lectionary (and obviously not everyone does), we have a new year of preaching ahead of us. A final thought here is that in this year that lies ahead, there is time enough for what needs to be preached. Across many denominations, there is a tendency to focus our preaching on certain texts: in the case of lectionary preachers, it is common to default to the Gospel reading more often than not, as if there was no time to focus on anything else. Compared to the reformed tradition that I stand in and the preaching traditions in which I was raised and formed, this kind of practical supersessionism is an unacceptable narrowing of the scope of preaching. To affirm that 'there is time' for preaching is to be ready for what an older homiletic text on my shelf calls 'planning a year's pulpit work'. It is to look out at the lectionary year and to say there is time for Luke, and for Romans, as well as for Deuteronomy, for Amos and for Job. In a 1983 lecture on 'Preaching the Old Testament' the biblical scholar Derek Kidner put it beautifully: 'Not every by-road leads to Doubting Castle; the King has His own quiet meadows and curious villages.'[3] (Put more prosaically, we should be wary of dismissing any part of the canon as a site for preaching.)

3 Kidner (1983); cf. Plantinga (2015), p. 1.

# 1.2 Naming the presence of God

## Learning from Sam Wells

When Christians gather together to worship, whether two or three or two or three thousand, they are quickly reminded or become aware of three things. The first is that they are in the presence of God. The ability to name the presence of God is a skill. It is a skill that the scriptures train the Church to perform.[1]

The practice of preaching, like other kinds of practice,[2] is informed and enabled by various kinds of 'know-how' and understanding. As preachers, we gather these from a rich range of sources, sometimes from a lecture, book or article on homiletics, sometimes from another theological or non-theological source, sometimes from observing others or reflecting on our own practice. Some of these insights we try hard to write on the walls of our own minds as reminders, others seem to imprint themselves. Throughout this book, I will be drawing attention to those that are most important to me as a preacher, and acknowledging their sources, since many come from other people.

One of the insights I return to most often, which has become central to how I think about worship and about the place of preaching within worship, is found in the quote at the beginning

---

1 Wells (2002), p. 67.
2 Bourdieu (1992).

of this chapter from Anglican theologian and minister Sam Wells. I recommend reading in full the article from which the quote is taken, but the key words for me were these: 'The ability to name the presence of God is a skill ... that the scriptures train the Church to perform.' It would be no exaggeration to say that these words changed my life; they certainly changed my work as a minister, liturgist and preacher, but they also changed my experience of reading Scripture. They did this not so much because they told me something I didn't know, but because they told me something I *did* know – but didn't *realise* I knew. Wells's words crystallised an understanding of what was going on when I and others worshipped, in a way I found – and still find – profoundly helpful and persuasive.

In the article, Wells fills out their meaning by speaking of how as worshippers, through Scripture, we 'enter a tradition of providence encompassing Noah's rainbow, Isaac's ram, Moses' pillar of cloud, Hannah's prayer, Daniel's lions, Elizabeth's child, the stilled storm, the Great Commission, the new Jerusalem'.

It will be obvious that, like Wells, I have a 'high' view of Scripture. The encounter with Scripture is central to my understanding of preaching. What Wells's words do is to construe the encounter with Scripture in a particular way, which for me is both beguilingly simple and endlessly rich. When I was an undergraduate, I learned to be zealous about defending the status of Scripture, but there was always a sense that I was being asked to 'protect' Scripture, by arguing for an extrinsic account of its authority. In the decades since then, the formal account I would give of the nature and status of Scripture has become more nuanced and qualified, but my reverence for Scripture and my expectation of the disclosive power of reading it has increased. One of my favourite quotes about the Bible comes from the pioneering translator of Scripture into contemporary English idioms, J. B. Phillips, who said that translating the Bible was like rewiring an ancient house with the electricity still connected to the mains.[3] I love that image of the live, sparking, dangerous text, which reminds me of Annie Dillard's often quoted passage about coming to church in a crash helmet.[4] It also introduces pneumatology to our engagement with the text, so we are encountering the Spirit as we encounter the word. This means that, as preachers, we approach the text with a spiritual expectancy. A key part of this is that through any particular passage we are expecting to be trained in the skill of naming the presence of God. Wells's unusual use of the words 'training' and 'skill', as well as showing his debt to Stanley Hauerwas and Alasdair MacIntyre, surprise us into recognising something that has already been going on within us, as a work of the Holy Spirit in our Christian formation.

When we specify further that the high view of Scripture we are advocating is also a 'broad' view, we move towards the theological traditions associated with the canon, thinking not just of canon as a limit concept,[5] but as a call to explore the bounds of Scripture and a promise that our encounter with all parts of the canon can be profitable for 'training in righteousness'.[6] As a critical concept, canon also helps us to reflect on how to work with parts of Scripture that we struggle with, or are shocked or confounded by – something I will say more about in Part 2 on 'Reading'. Canon in this sense is itself a *tradition* of naming the presence of God, where tradition is, in Alasdair MacIntyre's terms, 'an extended, socially embodied argument' about what that skill sounds like and feels like.[7] Canonical preaching extends and embodies that tradition in new places and times.

---

3  Phillips (1952), p. xii.
4  Dillard (1982), pp. 40–1.
5  Which of course it is.
6  2 Timothy 3:16–17.
7  MacIntyre (1981), p. 222.

## Customising worship and preaching

I believe that the encounter with the Scriptures set for any given day in the Christian year should be liturgically crucial for the act of worship within which preaching takes place. This alignment is already partly and even substantially there within traditions that use a missal or prayer book, but the pre-arranged character of this may only take us so far into any given contemporary context. Within my own reformed tradition, many of the prayers and responses within a service are composed or selected by those leading worship on a more ad hoc basis. Across all denominations, the selection of music and hymns/worship songs is usually done on a week-by-week basis, so within most churches there is scope for at least some *customisation* of worship and liturgy in any given service. I want to suggest eight forms that this customisation can take, all of which relate to the task identified earlier of finding the liturgical year, the lectionary year and the life year. In this way, Wells's wonderful insight about our being trained in the skill of naming God's presence can help us to understand more about how we are trained in that skill, and how we are called to use it. Such customisation is to be:

### 1 Seasonal

The different seasons of the Christian Year are distinguished by their association with particular scriptures, stories, images, doctrines and practices that thicken our understanding of how to name God, how to pray, sing and preach. We take our bearings from them, so that on any given day we are 'finding time' and knowing where we are within the year.

### 2 Scriptural

Our reading of the Scriptures trains us, but it does so week by week and scripture by scripture. Engaging with how God is imaged, named and encountered in the readings set or chosen for the day, we can use these examples and insights to shape our choice of hymns and songs, to customise our prayers and liturgical responses, and to influence how we name and construe God in the sermon.

## 3 Cultural

Liturgy and preaching needs to be culturally reflexive, self-aware and, so far as it can be, 'woke' or politically conscious and aware. Every liturgical and homiletical act and occasion is always inculturated, freighted with assumptions, references, allusions and illustrations; it is accented, embodied and clothed. So every worship service in every church is already culturally customised, with perhaps 90 per cent of this being unexamined, unplanned, unconscious. Critical reflection on inculturation will often need to be done in dialogue and conversation with other minds and bodies. I remember vividly as a twenty-year-old student being given a copy of Columbus Salley and Ronald Behm's *Your God Is Too White* by a black English colleague on the UCCF national executive in the early 1980s. It was a wake-up call and a warning that I badly needed, and that I recognise as a work of the Spirit in beginning to disciple my identity as a white man. Within a year I would find myself worshipping in a multicultural congregation in inner-city Hackney, in London and a decade or so later would be back there for seven years as pastor of a neighbouring congregation, half of whose worshippers would eventually be non-white. Thirty years later that journey continues – of trying to be aware of my own cultural accents, assumptions and exclusions as a preacher, of trying to understand the privilege and responsibility of preaching to culturally diverse congregations. What is true of my whiteness is also true of my maleness, of my middle-class identity, of my being straight. The same remedies apply: to welcome the fact that all of this needs to be discipled and to see it as a work of the Spirit in my life as a preacher; to apologise and seek forgiveness when I make mistakes; to collaborate

and listen and be open to critical reflection on my own practice. Growing in cultural awareness involves every preacher in
a lifelong journey of *metanoia*, of having our minds renewed,
our awareness raised, our practice changed.

As well as the kind of cultural awareness linked to issues of
diversity, preachers need to cultivate the broader *zeitgeisty*
awareness of cultural trends and moments, of how people's
lives are changing and why, of 'what's going on'.[8] One of the
great gifts missiology can bring to homiletics is a tradition of
cross-cultural awareness and reflection. The missiologist and
scholar of global Christianity Lamin Sanneh, in his seminal
book, *Translating the Message*, reminds us that whenever the
gospel is first translated, those learning the language from outside need someone else, a 'native speaker', to tell them the name
of God.[9] All of this is about naming God. Every act of naming
and proclaiming the gospel must and should be customised,
inculturated and contextualised, but to absolutise my own
culturally limited understanding is a form of blasphemy and
idolatry. Disciples are always learning to preach in new and
changing contexts; it's part of the preacher's job description.[10]

## 4 Ecological

Another massive horizon for homiletics in the twenty-first
century is ecological awareness. What does it mean for us
to speak in the name of the Creator in this situation? The
psalmist writes that 'Our help is in the name of the Lord,
the maker of heaven and earth'.[11] Pope Francis's 2015 papal
encyclical *Laudato sí* reminds the whole Church of the theo-

---

8 As Marvin Gaye puts it in the title song of his 1971 album (Tamla
Motown, 1971).

9 Sanneh (1989), p. 161.

10 'At any point in its history, the church needs both the confidence that it has
a gospel to preach and the ability to see that it cannot readily specify in advance
how it will find words for preaching in particular new circumstances' (Williams
(1999), pp. 29–43).

11 Psalm 124:8.

logical imperatives involved in ecological awareness and recalls Francis of Assisi's example in 'preaching to the flowers'.[12]

## 5 Political

There can be no faithful preaching that is not also politically aware: aware of the calls to justice and peace that sound throughout the Scriptures, aware of the political implications of divine sovereignty and the Lordship of Jesus Christ, aware of the material conditions of our neighbours near and far, and aware of the power relations and differentials of our own context. Bonhoeffer's famous insistence in Nazi Germany that 'Only he who cries out for the Jews may sing Gregorian chants'[13] could equally well end 'may preach a sermon in the Church'. In the spirit of Matthew 25, not to see the realities of injustice and oppression in the world is not to see Jesus Christ. The skill of naming God in worship and preaching cannot be decoupled from the capacity to name the political realities around us.

## 6 Functional

How we preach and pray and sing is also shaped by what we are doing in worship, in particular by whether we are baptising or sharing communion, but also by whether we are giving thanks for new life, preparing to bury or cremate our dead, or witnessing and blessing the marriage of two people. The work of preaching is inseparably bound up with the work of the Church, with its practices, with what it is doing in worship.

## 7 Pastoral

The customisation of worship must also, always, be done in the light of the pastoral charge that is given to the Church. William Still, one of the great Scottish evangelical leaders of the

---

12 *Laudato sí*, 11.
13 Bonhoeffer quoted in Bethge (1999), p. 512.

twentieth century, wrote in his short book called *The Work of the Pastor*, of the prime responsibility pastors have to feed their sheep with the Word.[14] This pastoral concern for their spiritual nourishment must always be accompanied by a holistic concern for their good, particularly when they are suffering, or ill, or bereaved. Preaching that is careless of pastoral dimensions, that does not adjust and attend to the joys and sorrows of a congregation, will not minister the love of God. If it speaks in the tongues of humans and angels, but speaks without love, it is only white noise.

## 8 *Existential*

I use the word here in its sense of 'concreteness' to mean preaching as it takes place here and now. All of the previous points about how to customise preaching are for the sake of this one – how the word is to be preached 'today'. This is, of course, the great caution about any attempt to simply dust down previous sermons, to take them off the shelf or the hard-drive. An encounter that had a profound and lasting effect on my own ministry was when in Northern Ireland, church leader Derek Poole told me how during the Troubles, if there had been a violent incident, people from his independent congregation would go to pray near to the site of the bombing or shooting. He said something that has never left me, 'When we go there, we ask ourselves, what name of God should we cry out in this situation?' These words, along with the quotation from Sam Wells (which I came across much later) at the beginning of this chapter, are in my mind every time I sit down to prepare a sermon or prepare to lead a service. Nothing of this is new. It's the old conjunction of text and context that lies at the heart of preaching. The job of the preacher and of those leading worship is to mediate between the long, deep rhythms of Scripture and tradition, and the need to speak, sing and pray 'in this situation'. Whenever we open our mouths to preach,

---

14 Still (1996).

the particular dynamics of our immediate context put the question to us of what name of God we cry out now, today – and why?

In the reflections that follow, I will expand on some of these points, but I wanted to gather them together at the start, to give a sense of the 'skills' we are being called to and trained in. I also wanted to reflect on how, while it is sometimes a whole book or extended argument that will shape us as preachers, it may also be a sentence or a phrase – one that distils so much homiletical and liturgical wisdom we will never be done with it. These two sentences, from Sam Wells and Derek Poole respectively, are always with me as a preacher:

'The ability to name the presence of God is a skill ... that the scriptures train the Church to perform.'

'What name of God should we cry out in this situation?'

# 1.3 What do you see?

## Knowing your place and time

In January 2016 I was invited to speak at a church weekend in Northern Ireland, for Belfast-based Fitzroy Presbyterian Church. The sessions I led were all to be based on texts from Jeremiah. I had preached at a morning service there in Belfast the previous year, but I was nervous about this assignment. The religious and cultural politics of Northern Ireland are not easy terrain for outsiders to negotiate. I sat and stared at Jeremiah 1 for a long time. The call vision/narrative is usually reassuring for us as preachers, lending us a study prayer for times of preparation: 'Ah, Lord GOD! Truly I do not know how to speak …' (Jer. 1:6). In response, the Lord reaches out a hand to touch Jeremiah's mouth, and says, 'I have put my words in your mouth' (Jer. 1:9). I had remembered that part of the passage more vividly than what comes next in verse 11: 'The word of the LORD came to me, saying, "Jeremiah, what do you see?"'

I sat and stared at those words for a while. Another of my maxims (or mantras) in theology and life for the past two decades has been the claim of Iris Murdoch that Stanley Hauerwas cites in his 1982 essay on 'Ethics and the pastoral task': 'we can only act in the world we see'.[1] It is a haunting, compressed and distilled piece of wisdom which, when it gets inside our heads, is also generative, expansive and interrogative. It tends towards

---

1 Hauerwas (1974), p. 69.

making us stop and think again about what we were about to say and do. Like a brooding detective in a Nordic Noir TV series,[2] we stare out of the window at our neighbourhood and wonder what we are missing.

If it is also homiletic wisdom – we can only *speak* in the world we see – then it prompts us in two ways. There may be a particular episode of sermon preparation, where we struggle with a particular text and wonder what we are not seeing about the world in which we are reading it. But this episode belongs within a longer formation of ourselves as readers and preachers, where the question of what we see, what we attend to, where we look, what we read, etc., is being lived out over years and decades. How many times, particularly in situations of oppression, have those in positions of privilege haplessly reproduced the Matthew 25 line, 'Lord, when did we see you?'

As my friend Anthony Reddie says, with a revolutionary patience white people do not deserve, in his book *Is God Colour-blind?*: 'if you say you "don't see colour", then you don't see me'.[3]

To be called to preach is to be called to see the world as clearly and honestly as we can. It involves an ongoing attempt, in the words of Burns, 'To see oursels as ithers see us',[4] but it also requires a willingness to see what other people see, not to look away from poverty or suffering or injustice or privilege. The seeing is important, because sermons turn seeing into words.

My realisation that I needed to 'see' Northern Ireland as I sat in Glasgow reading Jeremiah 1:11–13 shaped how I read the text:

---

2 *The Killing, The Bridge, Borderlands*, etc.

3 Reddie (2009).

4 From Robert Burns, 'To A Louse, On Seeing One on a Lady's Bonnet at Church' (1786).

[The Lord said] 'Jeremiah, what do you see?' And I said, 'I see a branch of an almond tree.' Then the LORD said to me, 'You have seen well, for I am watching over my word to perform it.' The word of the LORD came to me a second time, saying, 'What do you see?' And I said, 'I see a boiling pot, tilted away from the north.'

Reading with an eye to seeing helped me to focus on the image of God watching over the words 'to perform it'. The repeated question to Jeremiah added a sense of insistence – 'Keep looking!' I added a slide to my presentation showing an image of the cover of Seamus Heaney's 1975 collection of poetry *North*, creating an intertext with Jeremiah's seeing of the political situation of his day, where trouble was brewing in the north and spilling over across the land. Those who have eyes to see, see a God who is watching over the word, for its effects to grow like almond blossom appearing from a dry branch, like boiling water spilling from a pot, like violence blighting the land.

That seeing continued through our engagement with other texts in Jeremiah – chapter 6: 'This is not peace'; chapter 8: 'Cry me a river'; chapter 18: 'If God is against us'; chapter 19: 'I will break you'; chapter 29: 'To all the exiles'; chapter 31: 'Dry your tears'; chapter 31: 'A new covenant'; and chapter 32: 'Field of dreams'. As an outsider, I tried to be reticent and respectful, asking preacherly questions about how those in that Belfast congregation read the text, about what associations it raised for them – not trying to say more than I could see. Other local speakers on the programme spoke about the 100th anniversary of the Easter Rising and the Battle of the Somme and about the ongoing peace process. They could see more and differently than I could. When we were reading chapter 31 of Jeremiah, it became clear that, following the example of Matthew's Gospel, we tended to focus on verse 15 about Rachel weeping for her dead children and refusing to be

comforted – and then to effectively stop reading. For me as
a preacher, it was enough to keep us as a congregation reading on into verse 16: 'keep your voice from weeping and your
eyes from tears'. The sermon, even from an outsider such as
myself, could follow Jeremiah in raising the question about
the time to dry tears which comes after the weeping in Ramah.
The answers to that question, in a post-conflict situation like
Northern Ireland, were answers I could not see from the outside and did not presume to give.

We can only preach in the world we see. We preach as those
sent by a God who continually asks, 'What do you see?' Our
prayer as preachers is 'open our eyes, Lord'. It is what the
reformed tradition calls 'the prayer of/for illumination': 'Come,
Holy Spirit, help us to see … both Christ and the world.'

# 1.4 Who do you see?

## Learning from Andrew MacLellan

Books on preaching produced in Scotland have been in short supply in recent decades, but one – which was also a book *of* preaching – was the 1996 collection of sermons by Andrew McLellan, an Edinburgh minister who went on to be Moderator of the Kirk's General Assembly and then, more surprisingly, from 2002 to 2009, Her Majesty's Chief Inspector of Prisons in Scotland. The title of his book was *Preaching for These People*.[1]

McLellan's title captures something profoundly important about preaching, which is that it is a personal, communal and social practice. The word 'sermon' carries from its origins a sense of conversation, which has been recovered in some modern homiletical writing.[2] Whether or not we are 'preaching to the converted', we are always preaching *to* someone, to these women and men, these people, in all of their particularity. If we are preaching to people we know, this relationship is informed by knowing something of who they are and what they have been through. The pastoral customisation of preaching already mentioned *sees* the people in the congregation who have recently been bereaved, who have been struggling with depression, who are going through a third cycle of IVF treatment at great expense, who are about to get married, who have

---

1 McLellan (1996).
2 For example, Rose (1997).

just come out, who earn more than anyone else in the church. Preaching has to be saying things 'to people's faces', as we say in Scotland, in an everyday expression that resonates with the work of philosopher Immanuel Levinas. It has to do with how the other claims us, since the face of the other is Mount Sinai, is the Torah.[3] The face of the other is an ethical summons and an ethical challenge. Preaching is on dangerous ground when it is talking about people 'behind their backs'. The question of presence also implies other questions of exclusion and absence. Who is not here to hear and why?

Seeing the people in front of us, in all of their particularity and in their own common identities, also raises questions about how we speak to those who are not us. How do I as a man preach to women? How do I as a straight man preach to the LGBTI folk in a congregation? What does it mean for me as a white person to speak to people of colour? For me as an able-bodied person to speak to people with disabilities? How do I, as a middle-class professional, preach to those who are poorer than me, with less formal academic education? The example of Jesus is powerful here, as someone who – in the KJV rendering of Mark 12:37 – the common people 'heard gladly'. You could preach a whole sermon on that verse, but somewhere it would have to include reflection on how 'these people' felt they were being spoken to. Jesus was certainly willing to offend and to speak uncompromisingly, but the witness of the Gospels is to someone who was heard gladly by the poorest and most vulnerable, the outcasts and untouchables. As preachers, that is something we are discipled to.

When we see people and know something of their story, it shapes how we speak. It works against any glibness or insensitivity in how we speak about something that we know may cause them pain or anguish. We may not be able to avoid

---

3 Levinas (1985), pp. 85–9.

preaching on a topic that some will find hard to hear – both the scripture and the occasion may demand it – but we should have a feel for which words may sting and provoke.

I often show Paul Gauguin's famous 1888 painting *Vision After the Sermon* to students when lecturing on preaching.[4] I will return to this later, but for now I simply note that unless we leave by the vestry door and drive far away, there is also an 'after the sermon'. We are responsible for our words and they carry over into our relationships with those we preach to, including our own families (who are most likely to notice a discrepancy between a pulpit persona and the one they live with day to day). There is a living with 'these people' that helps to determine whether preaching *to* is also, in McLellan's phrase, a preaching 'for'. That living with, after the sermon, will often require explanation, dialogue, listening, pastoral care and visiting. It may sometimes require apology and reconciliation if we have mis-spoken (mis-preached?). On the positive side, where preaching is valued, is pastorally sensitive, and is appropriately challenging, it may enhance and support life after the sermon in ways that our hearers in a congregation are deeply grateful for.

---

4 The painting hangs in the National Gallery of Scotland, in Edinburgh.

# 1.5 Focus – what was the sermon about?

## Learning from Thomas Long

I said in the Introduction that because this book is an extended reflection on my own practice and experience as a preacher, there would be a steady acknowledgement of debts to those I have learned from. This section and several others take their bearings from the work of the influential homiletics scholar Thomas G. Long. In his acclaimed 1989 book *The Witness of Preaching*, Long introduced his pithy formula of 'focus and function'.[1] I will reflect on the 'function' part in section 1.6, but here I stay with 'focus'.

I said earlier that I often do not find books on homiletics particularly helpful, but Long is one of the exceptions. I have found his work consistently helpful, not least for its clarity and, in the best sense, simplicity. In *The Witness of Preaching*, Long was mediating between what he called the 'main idea crowd' and the 'aesthetic crowd' and seeking to bind together 'content and intention'.[2] 'Biblical texts *say* things that *do* things, and the sermon is to say and do those things too.'[3]

One of Long's gifts to preaching classes and to beginning homiletics students was his encouragement to write out formal

---

1 Long (1989), ch. 4, pp. 78ff.
2 Ibid., p. 85.
3 Ibid., p. 84.

'focus' and 'function' statements: 'A *focus statement* is a concise description of the central, controlling and unifying theme of the sermon. In short, this is what the whole sermon will be "about".'[4] Long's proposal was presented clearly and persuasively, with helpful examples of statements he judged to be too general, or too ambitious, or of where focus and function statements were misaligned with one another.

After three decades of preaching and a decade of teaching preaching, I still find Long's *via media* helpful. It needs to be subjected to various nuances and qualifications, many of which he already offered in his 1989 proposal, but it is helpful in identifying a basic tension to be kept – and doing this in a way that is memorable and pedagogically useful. Although it is not the only question worth asking, and it can be posed in ways that are reductive and one-dimensional, people do ask 'what was the sermon about?' and it is a sensible, meaningful and crucial question to ask. The years 2016–17 will be remembered as those in which 'post-truth' political discourse was named and shamed when it reached a certain apotheosis in the election of Donald Trump and the campaign for Brexit. This represented the most toxic legacy and the most bitter fruit of postmodernism, whose mixed legacy in politics and theology we are now picking our way through. The 'aboutness' of preaching is the intellectual and ethical pole of homiletics, which insists on the continuing importance of dogma, doctrine, truth and reference. It anchors not only the 'teaching' element of preaching, but the prophetic element also.

---

4 Ibid., p. 86.

# 1.6 Function – what was the sermon doing?

## Learning from Thomas Long

Having restated a commitment to the importance of focus in Thomas Long's pairing of focus and function, I want also to reinforce the importance of the second term. When considering this, it is rightly observed that people will most often ask 'what was the sermon about?' That is not going to change, but for preachers the question 'what is the sermon *doing*?' has been a massively important and helpful one in modern homiletics. Mennonite homiletician Allan Rudy-Froese identifies H. Grady Davis's 1958 book *Design for Preaching* as one of the first places where this (classic rhetorical) question was asked of the Protestant sermon in the twentieth century.[1]

The waves of new engagement with this question in homiletics over the past six decades have been driven by two other major currents running within Western intellectual life: *the linguistic turn* dating from the first half of the twentieth century[2] and *the literary turn* of the later twentieth century.

These currents focus on the constructive, performative functions of language, genre and textuality, paying fresh attention to intentionality, rhetoric and design, but also, particularly in later postmodern and poststructuralist moves, insisting on a

---

1 Rudy-Froese (2009).
2 Wesley Allen (2010), p. 5.

critical interrogation of how language is working and what texts are doing. They remind us that the operations and effects of language exceed the capacity of intentional operations of control and direction. When this sensibility goes into over-drive, however, it can seem impossible to stabilise meaning. The liberative 'intentions' of critical theory to expose relations of dominance, oppression and suppression within processes of reading and interpreting can become self-consuming and self-defeating. Necessary strategies of hermeneutical suspicion can too easily lead to methodological cynicism or solipsism.

Homiletics is still processing and negotiating its relationship to these turns, which have brought both indispensable insights and uncomfortable dilemmas to the work of preaching. I will say some more about these in my discussions of 'Reading' in Part 2. In Part 1, I am still trying to draw together and integrate a range of skills, practices and orientations that constitute our understanding of preaching.

An approach to preaching that asks questions about what the sermon is doing will have to operate with a mixed orientation of heightened attentiveness to form, and heightened suspicion about power. It will follow the literary turn towards a focus on the final, canonical forms of Biblical texts and will become more sceptical about the claims of historical and source criticism to access or reconstruct a world 'behind the text'. In attending to the texts as we have them, it will draw on the methods of literary criticism to enable a new attentiveness to genre, style, poetics and plot. In this way it will seek to attend to what Paul Ricoeur calls 'the world in the text'. It will be constantly asking questions about how the poetics of the text and the poetics of the sermon are to be related to one another.

This attentiveness to form will be accompanied by a more suspicious hermeneutical approach to how interpreters con-strue what is going on with the text, how they have understood and used the text, and to how I, as a preacher, am going to interpret/expound/perform the meaning of the text. In this way it will attend to 'the world in front of the text', a world which we have already acknowledged: all of us as interpreters/preachers need to consider our own locations, confess our own limitations and check our own privileges.

We do that not because we want to be, in a phrase I loathe, 'politically correct', but because we want to be good readers and good preachers, in both the technical and the ethical senses of those terms. The question about 'what the sermon is doing' has to also be addressed as a series of questions: What are we doing? What am I doing? and What is God doing? What will be telling will be the verbs we use to answer this question.[3] Our sermon may be comforting, it may be disturbing, it may be blessing, it may be unmasking. It may be warning, or lamenting, or protesting or interrogating.

As with our discussion of focus, talk of function leads inexorably to ethics, to the ethics of interpretation, of rhetoric, of proclamation. To cite Jeremiah again, he was conscious of those who were saying 'Peace, peace', when there was no peace (6:14).

It has to do with how we respond to the injunction of 2 Timothy 2:15, 'Do your best to present yourself to God as one approved by [him], a worker who has no need to be ashamed, rightly explaining the word of truth.'

---

3 Cf. section 2.7.

# 1.7 Take them to the table

Churches vary across and within denominations as to how regularly they celebrate communion/the Lord's Supper/the Eucharist.[1] I grew up with a weekly tradition and that is still my overwhelming preference, but in my own reformed tradition here in Scotland, the norm is only now becoming monthly, having been quarterly for centuries. The liturgical setting of preaching is important, and it makes a difference to preaching if we are to celebrate communion later in the service. As a script preacher, whenever I prepare a communion sermon I write at the bottom of my page, 'take them to the table'. This is another dimension to the question about 'what a sermon is doing'; in this context, it is also leading people towards their communion with God and with one another.

My awareness of where we are going together in the service shapes how I read the passage and how I reflect on it. I confess to having some theological allergies to 'pan-sacramentalism' and overuse of the term 'sacrament', so I also want to be careful about not twisting the text to make it all and always somehow 'about' communion. There is an art to building a bridge towards what happens next in the liturgy and a well-chosen hymn or song may also be an important part of that. Calvin's

---

1 Calvin wrote that 'We call it either "the Lord's Supper" or "the Eucharist" because in it we are both spiritually fed by the liberality of the Lord and also give him thanks for his kindness' (quoted in Gerrish (1993), p. 19). If we also add 'the breaking of bread' and 'Communion/Holy Communion' we can see how even the description of the liturgical action takes an approach to foregrounding one dimension of its meaning and significance.

practice was not to have a Great Entrance after the sermon, but to have the elements of bread and wine already upon the table and to preach 'over' them. Word and sacrament were to be presented together, each interpreting and confirming the other.

The classic 'catholic' elements of the liturgy, including the bare words of institution from Paul or any one of the Gospel accounts, provide their own framing of what the Scottish reformed tradition calls 'the action'. Within that frame, the taking of bread and wine has its own capacity to 'speak'; but alongside that, every celebration of the Supper has its own specific context, with these people, in this place, at this time. In ways we have already considered, that is also a cultural, political and economic context. The word that accompanies and precedes the Supper is shaped by and speaks to that context.

In his classic study of *Calvin's Preaching*, T. H. L. Parker discusses Calvin's 'high' view of both word and sacrament: 'When God sends his messengers to announce his will to us he at the same time gives such power that the effect is joined to the Word.'[2] Parker is clear that it was not simply being declared that God is a gracious God; 'in his Word God was being gracious in St Pierre and La Madeleine and St Gervais in May 1555 ... This is the language of revelation.'[3]

That lovely phrase of Parker's, 'God was being gracious', helps to connect word and sacrament in a single thought, as by the Holy Spirit God is being gracious to worshippers in both the word and the sacrament. Bonhoeffer said that 'Christ walks through the congregation as the Word'.[4] In both word and sacrament, Christ comes to be present and Christ speaks. Both are inexhaustible sources of grace for the Church. We are

2 Parker (1992), p. 28.
3 Ibid., p. 29.
4 Fant (1975), p. 126.

never done with learning or perceiving or understanding how God is being gracious to us through the word and the sacrament. Every celebration of the Supper is a unique conjunction of people, word, sign and context. Every preaching where the table is set for the Supper is a new opportunity to thicken and deepen our understanding of what it means to be in Christ, to receive Christ, to follow Christ today.[5]

5 Jean-Jacques von Allmen says, 'The preaching of the Word has in fact always a sacramental purpose, it ever seeks as its end a sacrament which can confirm and seal it, or rather which will prove that it has borne fruit. If it is non-liturgical missionary preaching, it aims at the sacrament of baptism; if it is parochial, liturgical preaching, it is orientated towards the Eucharist' (von Allmen (1965), p. 144). (I am indebted to Ron Rienstra, whose doctoral work refers to von Allmen, for this reference.)

# 1.8 Take me to the water

Preaching at a baptismal service will be a less common event in most churches, across all denominations, but many of the things I have just written about preaching at communion apply in the same way and for the same reasons.

There are some obvious differences though. No one gets any special treatment at communion; as Brian Wren's liturgy of invitation says so powerfully, 'at this table all are fed'.[1] There are no special *dramatis personae* here, because we are all sitting down together. (Even if some are still waiting to join in the eating and drinking, that is a waiting together with others, just as the eating and drinking is a partaking with others.) A baptism is different. Someone – or some people – are to be baptised and it is right that their journeys, their stories and their identities are recognised in the service. This is not to the exclusion of anyone else, but rather the personalising of some parts of the address should be a reminder and a witness to everyone of God's call to each of us in baptism. That someone else is named in this liturgy and sermon is not a forgetting of you or me, but a reminder of that time when we were each so named, or an invitation for us to be so named in the future.

If we think this through the genre of call and response, it's as if the congregation are singing the spiritual 'Take me to the water, to be baptised'[2] as a call to the preacher and to all those

---

1 Quoted in Morley (2004).
2 African American Spiritual – no. 480 in *Glory To God*, PCUSA Hymnal.

leading the worship, as well as a call upon God and an invocation of the Holy Spirit. The preached word forms part of the response to that call and constitutes part of the 'taking' of the candidate to the water.

The baptismal sermon, like the event of baptism itself, is a means of grace. The God who is going to be gracious to Kirsty or Fergus, Emmanuel or Nina in the water (and through the invocation of the triune name) is the same God who is first being gracious to them in the word that takes them there. For those, most of those attending, who will not literally get wet the word takes them to their identity as baptised people, or calls them to that identity.

For those being baptised as believers, on profession of their faith, this may also mark an early sign of their own participation in the Church's preaching ministry. As they give or share testimony, as they find and take voice in front of the assembly before going into the water, they share in the ministry of the word, the work of bearing witness. The designated or ordained preacher should be glad to make room for them, to enable them to be heard.

For the wider congregation, this is also a summons to be family, to be community, to be church to those being baptised on that day. This is true, whether the one being baptised is six weeks old, sixteen or sixty years old. The sermon calls the whole congregation to gather around the water and around those being baptised. It reminds them of the reasons why they need to be there: that these ones named and soaked need sisters and brothers to weep and rejoice with them, to bear their burdens, to forgive their sins, to encourage and support them. If we, like Christ, know ourselves as beloved of God in the act of baptism, then we should also know ourselves as being welcomed into what Martin Luther King Jr called 'the beloved community'.

# 1.9 When we come to die

I grew up in the Exclusive wing of the Darbyite Plymouth Brethren, and was a young child in the 1960s during the period of degeneration and division that has now been powerfully described by Rebecca Stott in her 2017 memoir, *In the Days of Rain*. As our little Brethren meeting journeyed further into 'separation from the world' and then –from the early 1970s – slowly re-emerged blinking into the light, one of the few times when there were outsiders at our worship was at funerals. Friends in Baptist and Pentecostal churches tell me that they too shared the experience of preachers in funeral services or at the graveside, eager to move from words related to the deceased, to turn and address the outside mourners, neighbours or work colleagues perhaps, who were presumed to be 'unsaved' – 'And if there is anyone here who doesn't know the Lord as their own personal Saviour, I know Jim/Helen/Donald would have wanted me to ...' If all preaching is a difficult privilege, preaching at funerals is more so, on both counts: more difficult, more of a privilege.

You will not be surprised to read that I deplore that kind of swivel-eyed evangelism at a funeral and that I believe it obscures rather than reveals the gospel, which should most definitely always be proclaimed at every Christian funeral service. Within the 'book liturgy' of my own church and of most churches that have service books, whatever their status,[1] the

---

1 In the Church of Scotland, our Books of Common Order are approved, not mandated.

key gospel proclamation will be made by the graveside or in the crematorium before the Committal and it often comes from the words of Jesus to Martha in John 11:25: 'I am the resurrection and the life; he who believes in me, though he die, yet shall he live and whoever lives and believes in me shall never die.' The 'do you believe this?' which Jesus puts to Martha in that context need not be put to the mourners gathered at the funerals where we preach. Death itself puts that question powerfully to all of us, when as the ancient liturgical prayer puts it, 'in the midst of life, we are in death'.[2]

Our task as preachers, above all, is to proclaim the hope of resurrection in those words of Jesus. There are other things to be said and done in funeral liturgies, whether scripted or improvised, but this is the most important. As Christians, we bury or cremate our dead, with the hope of the resurrection sounding in our ears, and as preachers it is our job to proclaim it.

My dear friend Ali called me from London in February 2007. She had been ill for several years and now had a terminal diagnosis. She also had a husband, Chris, who had been my ministry colleague in Hackney, and two children under five. 'You know what I'm going to say – I want you to preach at my funeral.' It was a fairly brief conversation. There was no way I was going to refuse and we were both too choked to say much. She died during Holy Week 2007 and this is the sermon I preached at her funeral on Friday 13 April, in The Round Chapel, Clapton Park United Reformed Church:

> Dear friends and neighbours, brothers and sisters, in what I say I am not going to speak so much about Ali's life and work – that has already been beautifully done by Chris and Sue, and will be continued later in the service by Neil and Lynda.

---

2 *Media vita in morte sumus.*

Ali phoned me back in February and asked if I would help to lead this service and if I would preach at it, and we also talked about today during a precious weekend we spent together in Binham just four weeks ago. What God has laid upon my heart to share with you this afternoon are some thoughts about what we in the Church have to say in response to Ali's death – what we say to God, and to one another, and to our neighbours and friends from beyond the Church: those of other faiths and none who are here today because of their respect and love for Ali and for Chris.

What *do* we have to say? What is there to say? It's not easy to find words in the face of death. Those who have been bereaved sometimes tell of others who find it hard to meet their eye – they just don't know what to say. We are looking for words which ring true – words that will not seem empty or trite or pointless. In the face of death all of us, preachers included, sense that our words can so easily turn to ashes in our mouths. And we are not wrong in feeling that. God save us from breaking the silences which need to be kept in our lives. If you knew Ali, you know she loved to talk – but she also knew how to keep silence with others.

But she believed there were things to be said today – things to be said and sung and prayed. And God save us too from keeping silent when there are things to be said.

Within the Church, as we look to the Scriptures, as we listen again for God's word to us, we find that there are things to be said even when, and especially when, as the Prayer Book says, 'in the midst of life we are in death'.

The first thing to be said is that 'it hurts' – it hurts like hell to lose someone we love so much – it hurts for a husband to lose his wife; for kids to lose their mum; for parents to lose a daughter; for a brother and sister to lose a sister; for friends to lose a friend. It hurts and it will hurt for a long time to come. Sometimes in the Church, in the midst of the other things we want to say, we have not said this strongly enough. But if we look to our Scriptures we find there are deep traditions of lament – of words and tears and sighs and groans; Israel crying out to God; Rachel weeping and refusing to be comforted; David falling to the ground weeping; Jesus weeping at the tomb of his friend Lazarus; Mary weeping on her way to Easter. Reflecting on this, a writer that Ali and Chris loved, Walter Brueggemann, says 'only grief permits newness'. Creation groans – we lament – we say that it hurts – and we demand that our hurt is heard by God – it hurts to lose Ali.

In our hurt and grief, we are also here to say 'thank you'. How could we not say thank you for so rich a life – for a life filled to the brim and overflowing with colour and laughter, with passion and compassion, with care and commitment. How could we not say thank you to the Maker for such a gift – for such a child, for such a lover, for such a sister. We are grateful to God for Ali's life and work – her work as an artist, her work as an activist, her work as a preacher and worship leader, her work as an elder, her work carrying and bearing and caring for children, her work persuading GPs to talk to one another – all of her work and all of her play – there is a stunning patchwork of memories – walks and meals and meetings and parties – long long conversations, songs sung together in church and at the table. Today we want to say thank you to God for Ali.

And as we say thank you – all the more insistently we have to say 'Why?' Why such loss and pain? Why only forty years? Why should this cruel disease of cancer rob us of so much life and love? Why so much potential unrealised? And for us within the Church – the hardest question of all, the one little Asha put to Chris – why doesn't God do what we ask him to?

Never trust a Christian who doesn't wrestle with God – they don't know their Bible and they don't know themselves. And lest we forget, Ali was not such a Christian – Ali's faith was real and deeply held, but it was not a brittle, shallow thing – she was a wrestler and a struggler – she knew that week by week she gathered to worship God in a broken and hurting world – in calling us to give to WaterAid and Armonia, she was reminding us that she too lived with asking why – she prayed with her eyes open to the things that make us want to do what Job's friends urge him to do in the Bible in the face of cruel suffering – to curse God and die in despair. She lived with unanswered questions – she could not explain any more than any of us can how Good Friday takes us to Easter Sunday – but she had found in the story of the crucified and risen Saviour the story on which she built all her hope. Some of us read the suffering of the world through other stories and she respected that – she knew that there is a profound human solidarity in asking why – but even as she held her questions and wrestled with God, she could say with Paul 'I know whom I have believed and am persuaded that he is able to keep that which I have committed unto him.'

For the Church, in holding that question 'why?' alongside the story of Jesus Christ, it becomes clear that there is another word to be said – it is the Easter word in which the Church proclaims God's Yes to life and finds God's No to death. We do not say death is nothing at all – we feel the sting of death and we rebel against it. Death is the last enemy, our Scriptures say, and one day death will die. We are Easter people and we will not make peace with death, because we believe what Paul's great cosmic vision in Romans 8 points to – that one day creation will be liberated from its bondage to decay. One day death will be overtaken by resurrection. I wrote this sermon in Catherine's kitchen in Roding Road – and pinned to the fridge beside me were these words from Dr Martin Luther King:

One day, youngsters will learn words they will not under-
stand. Children from India will ask what is hunger?
Children from Alabama will ask what is racial segregation?
Children from Hiroshima will ask, what is the atomic
bomb?
Children at school will ask what is war?
You will answer them, You will tell them, These words are
not used any more, like stage-coaches, galleys or slavery –
words no longer meaningful.
That is why they have been removed from the dictionaries.

And if we dare add to those prophetic words of Dr King, we
might add one day, we will say – in the words of Revelation
– death too will be a word we will no longer use or even
remember – because there will be no more dying there.

That 'no' to death is framed within another thing we dare to
say today. Here perhaps for many of us within the Church
our voices drop to a whisper – we worry that we will seem
childish or simple – still stuck in the pictures and stories of
Sunday school. I know that feeling well, but today I want to
raise my voice and say it loud – we say to Ali, *this is where you
are*, to one another *this is where she is*. In faith we speak of
things we cannot see – we gather up the brightest fragments
of material we find in the Scriptures and we piece together a
patchwork vision of heaven – of paradise, of 'iparidisi'. And
when we say to Asha and Kirin and to ourselves – when we
speak of Ali and say this is where she is – we point to different
pieces of this patchwork – we say – you have gone home –
you are in glory – now you live in a country called no more
death, no more crying, no more pain – and we are comforted.
We say – with the eyes of Narnia – you with your love for
life, you have said 'goodbye shadowlands, the term is over
and all the holidays have begun' – now you are where every
beauty is brighter and every pleasure more intense – you are
seated at the great feast – the ultimate community meal – you

are where there is the best wine, the finest food, the funkiest music, the brightest clothes, the wildest dancing, the kindest laughter, the deepest joy. Life is more where you are. And we are excited.

We say, with the jeweller's eyes of Revelation 21 – you, Ali, the magpie girl who loved stuff that glittered and sparkled and shone – you live now in the city whose walls are set with jasper, sapphire, agate, emerald, onyx, carnelian, chrysolite, beryl, topaz, chrysoprase, jacinth, amethyst – where the gates are pearls and the streets are pure gold, transparent as glass. And we are dazzled.

We say, with a mind to the sceptical Marxists among us and within us – to talk this way of heaven is no opiate – it is not spiritual heroin or crack which will drug us into oblivion – wherever the Church has fought hardest for justice and liberation down through the centuries – it has done so because it dreamed of heaven and it prayed for heaven's kingdom to come now on earth. We say with the voice of Dr King still ringing in our ears – this is where you are – Ali who adopted Hackney and loved living here – you are where there is every tribe and tongue and nation – where every language is spoken and every colour and culture fully respected. You are where every oppression is ended and every potential fulfilled. This is where you are and this is where we want to be – as Gabi sang – one day we will follow you. And for now – this vision does not dull our senses – eternity does not make a profit at time's expense – our vision of heaven urges us on to work for the kingdom here and now. You are where Jesus is and in the Spirit so are we – and every day, every Eucharist, we are in living communion with you and with all the saints in glory. We see through a glass darkly – but you see face to face.

If I have taken time to say this – it is because I have Ali's example before me – and it is because I believe these things should be said. Today we are having church – and as Christ's church we have things to say in the face of death. We say, it hurts, we say thank you, we ask why, we say no to death, we say this is where you are. There are two more things to be said – we turn to Chris and Asha and Kirin – remembering how a week ago today we heard Christ's words to John and Mary from the cross – son, behold your mother, woman behold your son – words which reshaped a broken family – we say to you, Ali's beloved Chris – we are here for you – we are your family – we will stay with you through this brokenness and loss.

The final thing which needs to be said – we will say to Ali as we close this service – because today we also have to say goodbye – goodbye to the body in which you loved us and we loved you – goodbye for now to the living up-close presence which enlivened our lives – we say goodbye, dear Ali, may God hold you safe in the palm of his hands.

All that we say, to God, to one another, and to Ali, we say now in the name of the Father and of the Son and of the Holy Spirit, Amen.

# 1.10 God be in my mouth

This final reflection on preaching in Part 1 takes on a thought we have already been working with in the previous two reflections on preaching and the sacraments: the highest possible claim that can be made for preaching is that it can be a form of the word of God. In a 2009 essay on 'The Theology of Worship', David Fergusson refers to Bullinger's famous dictum that 'the preaching of the Word of God *is* the Word of God':

> This was a marginal note added to the text of the *Second Helvetic Confession – praedicatio verbi Dei est verbum Dei* – reflecting Bullinger's belief in the power of the proclaimed message, even when announced by unworthy ministers … This message, however, always has a derivative and dependent status in relation to Scripture. It does not merely proclaim the message of the Bible but interprets it for a given time and place, so that it becomes again the Word of God. Expounded in Bullinger's *Decades*, this became something like the standard Reformed view. It establishes the centrality of proclamation in the life of the church while also insisting upon its subordination to the written Word.[1]

Bullinger's claim was reaffirmed in his own distinctive theological accents by Karl Barth, whose understanding of the threefold form of the word of God, extended from revealed and written to include 'preached'.[2]

---

1 Fergusson in Forrester and Gay (2009), p. 76.
2 See Barth (1975), 1.1.4, p. 88; McCormack (1909–36), pp. 340–1; Currie (2013); Barth (1928).

Barth's handling of this difficult claim negotiates its way through the obvious reservations and difficulties we might have with it. The human work of study and preparation is neither irrelevant nor sufficient. What undergirds the event of human preaching becoming the word of God is the decision and act of God the Holy Spirit, taking up human words and actions that are not adequate to this end. God chooses to speak through our human speaking, to make that which is not the word of God become the word of God. This is something that can only be enabled and secured from God's side.

If we affirm Bullinger's dictum, whether by Barth's method or some other, we have grounds for both *hope* and *humility* in our preaching. We offer our work of bearing witness, of expounding the word and proclaiming the gospel in the hope that God will use it. We recognise, however, that on its own this work is weak, partial and flawed, limited by both our finitude and our fallenness, and this should be a cause of great humility on our part.

Such a 'high' – or some would say 'sacramental' – view of preaching comes with caveats to preachers and to hearers. Preachers must continually seek to remember and understand that this possibility for preaching only exists because of the Holy Spirit, and so they are endlessly repeating the *epiclesis* – 'God be in my mouth'. Both preachers and their hearers must resist the temptation to identify the possibility of God speaking through preaching with their own rhetorical skill or capacity, with the 'success' of their preaching in promoting church growth, or with the recognition and acclamation of their preaching by others – though always also without making those things irrelevant or unimportant.

This is a dimension of preaching that we can also bear witness to from our own experience. As someone who has been extensively involved over the years in innovative work done under the rubric of 'alternative worship' or 'emerging church', I have often been struck by the hostility to preaching among friends and co-workers in these settings. Some of them expressed bafflement and even hostility at the idea that I was writing a book on preaching. It was as if I had announced I was writing a book commending theological 'mansplaining'. I do hear their voices, and in some respects I take their point. There are many ways in which the worship and life of the Church needs to change and develop and preaching is certainly one of them. My own witness, however, must also be to the reality of having felt myself addressed by God through preaching and to the sense of an excess, an abundance, of there being something *more* carried by the preacher's words, which I have known and received as the presence and power of God at work in my life. To this I would have to also add, although it is harder to speak of, the sense of my own words being carried into the congregation to be more than I could have intended or aimed them to be.

# PART 2

# Reading

# 2.1 On learning to read

In Part 2 of this book, I want to spend time reflecting on the role that 'reading' plays in preaching. It has been my own experience that a great part of learning to preach, or of the learning I have done so far, has been about learning to read. It has also been my experience, as someone who teaches a preaching class, that much of what shapes, limits and inhibits the work of preaching is the capacity of students to read and engage with Scripture.

Augustine, in the Confessions, famously describes hearing himself summoned *'tolle, lege'* – take and read. One of the most memorable modern theological discussions of reading is found in the 1991 book *Theological Hermeneutics* by my former Glasgow colleague, Werner Jeanrond. Jeanrond suggests that just as Schleiermacher described understanding as an 'art', we can also describe reading in this way – in other words, as a particular form of understanding.[1] To read, for Jeanrond, is to interpret, and all acts of reading are interpretative acts[2] in which the reader has to re-create the sense of a text.[3]

One of Jeanrond's most original contributions here is to suggest that just as there are genres in writing/text-production, so there are genres of reading/text-reception.[4] Jeanrond considers

---

1 Jeanrond (1991), p. 93. I recommend this book and Chapter 5, The Transformative Power of Reading, within it.
2 Ibid.
3 Ibid., p. 94.
4 Ibid.

how contemporary theories of reading operate along a spectrum, between the two poles of determinism and relativism, illustrated for him by the work of E. D. Hirsch and Roland Barthes.[5] He suggests that both distort the dialectic between text and reading, with Hirsch denying the 'productive' role of reading, while Barthes limits 'the effect of the text' on the reader.[6]

Naming reading as a socio-political, psychological and cultural activity, Jeanrond summons philosophers Derrida, Foucault and Ricoeur to deconstruct, unmask and reconsider what is going on when we read.[7] Derrida and Foucault are seen in various ways to expose both the power and the fragility of the reading self, introducing new levels of suspicion and self-doubt into our understanding of ourselves as readers.[8] Jeanrond suggests that Paul Ricoeur helps us to understand reading as an existential activity, which has a transformative power, but in which we ourselves are also in question and in process.[9] In response to this, we are called to 'an ethics of reading', in which our critical and dialogical belonging within an open and public community of readers and interpreters helps both to protect texts from us and to protect us from texts.[10] Jeanrond emphasises our limits as readers and argues that the wisest goal is to work for a 'relative adequacy'.[11]

Many of the points Jeanrond makes are also made by James K. A. Smith in his succinct and accessible 2006 work *Who's Afraid of Postmodernism – Taking Derrida, Loyotard and Foucault to Church*.[12]

---

5  Ibid., p. 95.
6  Ibid., p. 97.
7  Ibid., pp. 102ff.
8  Ibid., pp. 105–7.
9  Ibid., p. 110.
10  Ibid., p. 117.
11  Ibid.
12  Smith (2006); for a fuller treatment of hermeneutics, see Smith (2012).

While Jeanrond is interested in a general phenomenology of reading that is, reflecting on what is going on when everyone or anyone reads anything, he also reflects on what we mean by theological hermeneutics or theological reading. Another key section in this significant book, offers an insightful comparison of the theological hermeneutics of Barth and Bultmann, again (as with the philosophers) drawing on Paul Ricoeur to offer a third way. With Ricoeur's support, both Barth's 'macro-hermeneutics' and Bultmann's 'micro-hermeneutics' are criticised for taking (different) short cuts to theological interpretation.[13] In his 1994 Finlayson Lecture, also citing both Ricoeur and Jeanrond, Kevin Vanhoozer accused both Charles Hodge and Rudolf Bultmann in their different ways of using 'flattening' hermeneutics and, in a memorable phrase, 'refusing to walk the contours of the text'.[14]

What the work of Ricoeur, Jeanrond and Vanhoozer calls us to is a disciplined and attentive reading – what Ricoeur calls 'the long road to interpretation'.[15] With Jeanrond and Smith, I believe that while we may now (gratefully) have passed peak postmodernism and post-structuralism, we can also be grateful for the ways in which our practice as readers was shaped by those unsettling, suspicious and playful times.

I know that as someone raised within fundamentalist – then evangelical – Christianity, I was a highly defensive reader, fiercely protective of the text, but my exposure to post-structuralism was a way – I believe the Holy Spirit's way – of helping me to see how those instincts often effectively stopped me from reading. You could say that Derrida and Foucault taught me to read, and did so in ways that I believe have made me a better preacher.

---

13 Ibid., pp. 129ff.

14 This was a verbal aside in the course of delivering the sections found at pp. 106–7 of Kevin J. Vanhoozer's 1994 Finlayson Lecture (Vanhoozer, 1994), pp. 96–124.

15 Quoted in Jeanrond (1991), p. 145.

## 2.2 What are you reading?

How we read is influenced decisively by what we think we are reading. Here I want to offer some brief reflections on three ways of answering that question. The first, in line with what was said in Part 1 about having a 'high' view of Scripture, has to do with how we understand and receive the Bible as a gift from God and how we believe God speaks to us through the Bible. This raises huge questions, about which there is already a vast and ever-growing literature. My reflections here are more personal and practical than systematic or dogmatic. I have already described some of the story of my journey with the Bible: moving away from a more defensive and protective stance to a more open and exploratory one, and also moving from a tightly defined theory of Biblical authority to a more nuanced and qualified understanding. There is a personal spiritual journey that has gone along with that. Moving away from my defensive instincts has deepened my sense of trusting in the Holy Spirit to guide my reading.

Moving towards a less formulaic notion of Biblical authority has been accompanied by a deeper sense of how God speaks to the world and the Church through Scripture. Becoming more aware of the limiting and distorting effects of my own economic, cultural, political and social presuppositions has been for me a call of the Holy Spirit to *metanoia*. When I read the Scriptures now, more than at any other time in my life, I do so with a sense of hope and humility and with an expectancy that God will speak to me and others through our encounter with them. It is my testimony that even the most vigorous and deconstructive operations I have seen performed on the Biblical texts have not moved me away from being willing to affirm with Barth that this is the written word of God. I continue to believe it makes all the difference to us as preachers what we think we are reading. If we believe, in some sense, that the Holy Spirit is committed to helping us read and speak about these texts, before and above all others, that conviction will be decisive for our practice.

The second reflection on what we are reading is that it was remembered, written and handed down 'at sundry times and in diverse manners'[1] by human beings. The Bible is a very human book, whose divine inspiration has not overridden or over-written a whole host of historical, cultural, scientific, political and theological limitations. The 'relatively adequate' reading of it we aspire to therefore requires that we read canonically, that we read critically, and that we read within a community of critical theological dialogue and enquiry. It requires that we read as praying disciples of Jesus Christ, seeking the guidance of the Holy Spirit as we within the Church make judgements about how to respond to areas where the wording of specific scriptural texts is in tension with what we believe the Spirit is calling us to believe, and to do, in our time. This is not a new task for the Church. It was faced by Peter in the house of Cornelius, and by Paul, in arguments with the 'Judaisers', as both went on a journey of transformed understanding about law, covenant, and who belonged to the people of God. It was faced by John Calvin as he tried to draft hermeneutical criteria for which parts of the Old Testament law applied to Christians in sixteenth-century Europe. It was faced by African–Americans fighting to end slavery in the eighteenth and nineteenth centuries and to gain civil rights in the twentieth century, and also by women campaigning for ordination and against discrimin-

---

1 The famous KJV rendering in Hebrews 1:1.

ation in the nineteenth and twentieth centuries. It is an ongoing challenge for churches around the world today, as they wrestle with hermeneutical questions around LGBTI issues. Preachers in every era of the Christian Church find themselves in messy, compromised and contested situations, in which they have to do their best – and in which they often fail. Thank God, some preachers manage to speak with prophetic and luminous clarity on certain issues at key moments. No preachers speak rightly about everything, all the time. We may (and should) pray 'God be in my mouth', but we will look around and look back to see that, in the mouths of others and in our own preaching mouths, there was also confusion, prejudice, ignorance, oppression and fear. As we read in James 3:1–2, 'Not many of you should become teachers, my brothers and sisters, for you know that we who teach will be judged with greater strictness. For all of us make many mistakes.'

My final reflection on what we are reading focuses on the question of literary genre. One of the key books that has shaped me as a preacher is Thomas Long's fairly short 1989 volume, *Preaching and the Literary Forms of the Bible*.[2] The point to be made here is actually a fairly simple one,[3] but one that still seems to often be more honoured in the breach than the observance. Long simply urges us as readers to pay close attention to the literary genres of the parts of the Bible we are reading as we prepare to preach. Again, the issue is about learning to read. There are both theological and practical ways of pre-loading expectations about 'what we are reading' that seem to fuel a genre blindness within us: the categories of Scripture and sermon separately and together can work to obscure and efface the literary forms. My friend, the poet, novelist and photographer Harry Smart, talks with a wry, self-deprecating wit about his early experiences working with evangelical student groups,

---

2 Long (1989).
3 As Long points out (Long, 1989), p. 11.

which were intensely serious about Bible study, but were confounded by the realisation that so much of the Bible was in the form of 'poetry'. He grinned as he described the awkwardness accompanying the collective realisation by a group of earnest male evangelicals, raised on theories of 'propositional revelation', that it might have something to do with engaging 'our emotions'![4] Long wrote of the 'textual poetics' being 'commonly washed out in the typical text-to-sermon process', arguing that:

> An unfortunate result of overlooking the literary properties of biblical texts is the tendency to view those texts by default as inert containers for theological concepts. The preacher's task then becomes simply throwing the text into an exegetical winepress, squeezing out the ideational matter and then figuring out homiletical ways to make those ideas attractive to contemporary listeners.[5]

With this 'squeezing' metaphor, we are not far away from Vanhoozer's already noted observation about 'flattening' hermeneutics.

I noted earlier Long's skill in developing simple questions that are very helpful to those learning to preach, and he does not disappoint here, offering four key questions to bring to any given passage or reading:

### Genre questions
1 What is the genre of the text?
2 What is the rhetorical function of this genre?
3 What literary devices does this genre employ to achieve its rhetorical effect?

---

4 Personal communication from Harry Smart. See his collections of poetry, *Shoah*, *Pierrot* and *Fool's Pardon*, all published by Faber.
5 Long (1989), p. 12.

### Text question

How in particular does this text, in its own literary setting, embody the characteristics and dynamics in 1–3 above?[6]

I will return to this book by Long and these insights in Part 3 on speaking. Reflecting on my own experience, inserting these genre questions into the space between Scripture and sermon has had more influence on how I 'read for preaching' than almost anything else.

---

6 Long (1989), p. 24.

# 2.3 Are you expository?

In the evangelical reformed tradition that shaped me, after I had left the Exclusive Brethren, few things were so revered as 'consecutive expository' preaching. Some of this was with good reason. I still look back to hearing some of the leading preachers in this tradition with a certain awe and a deep sense of the impact their preaching made upon me. They all followed the old reformed pattern of reading and preaching sequentially through a whole book (consecutive), having no truck with 'lectionaries'. The other descriptor, 'expository', is a rich and potentially complex term. A staple of conservative literature on homiletics is the relationship between *exegesis* and *exposition* that lies at the heart of 'Biblical preaching'.

I am not setting myself up to pick a fight with either of these terms and I think they can still have continuing and helpful currency within homiletics. There are some well recognised concerns however, about how they are often used and understood, that ought to be acknowledged and recognised.

They are associated in church culture with a high view of Scripture and its authority, and with a conviction that for preaching to be 'of God's word' and 'under God's word', the content of preaching must be controlled and determined by the content of Scripture. The cautions arise for me, ironically, when readers of the Biblical texts operate with an insufficiently robust (and reformed!) view of how both our finitude and our fallenness affect our capacity to read and understand. Sin screws up our ability to read well. Hermeneutics and homiletics need to recognise this and take account of it in their methods. My concern about many iterations of how 'exegesis/exposition' works in preaching is that they operate with an objectivist, or what Jeanrond calls a 'determinist', view of hermeneutics. Instincts to defend truth, to protect and defend Scripture and to police heresy, are strong drivers of both theory and practice here, and again I am not in principle picking a fight with those things. I think it is important to detect and avoid heresy. I also think it is extremely important to work hard at all the 'technical' aspects of hermeneutics, grammar, vocabulary, alternative translations, figures of speech, metaphors, etc. I agree too that sermons shouldn't simply consist of *exegesis*, but that there are bridges of understanding, illumination and application to be built between the world of the text and the world of the congregation.

My concern, and there is nothing original or novel about it, is that this pervasive anxiety about control, defence and policing leads to positing an 'objectivist' model of hermeneutics, which is not true to how we read and interpret texts. This gives too thin an account of how we misconstrue and misinterpret texts, it tends in practice towards the methodological flattening of genre we have just been considering, and it fails to call us to a proper *metanoia* as readers and interpreters, because its objectivist concerns prevent us from cultivating a properly critical subjectivity. All of these are themes and concerns that run through this book. I offer this, then, not as a rejection of expository preaching, but as a health warning for how we engage in it.

# 2.4  On having (and being) a hermeneutic

My first ten weeks of academic theology were taught by Lesslie Newbigin, who was a visiting lecturer at the University of Glasgow. His lectures were subsequently published as *The Gospel in a Pluralist Society* and I highly recommend them. One of the justly famous phrases in that book, which has been widely quoted and which I vividly remember him saying to us, is his description of 'the congregation as the hermeneutic of the gospel'.[1]

When we use the term hermeneutic in the singular (and I will return to Newbigin's sense), it most often has a phenomenological sense; that is, we are trying to describe something about the operations of our own understanding, about how we 'read' texts and contexts.[2] A hermeneutic is a stance – how we face the text, how we lean into it – or we could see it as a kind of interpretive compass, allowing us to take our bearings in the textual landscape. It is a condensed set of assumptions and expectations about how things are, about what God and the good are like, about what constitutes orthodoxy or oppression. Some of this is highly self-conscious, but other parts sit below the surface of our consciousness, operating on a more instinctive level, so that we could also say a hermeneutic is a set of instincts we bring to a text, some of which are unrecognised or poorly understood.

1  Newbigin (1989). The whole of chapter 18 is devoted to this theme
2  In this sense, it has a lot in common with the idea of a 'paradigm'.

In some ways, having a hermeneutic is like having an accent. We all have one and we all find it hard to hear our own. We become most conscious of our own in situations of difference, particularly when we are in a minority, so that we stand out to others and to ourselves, or when we have difficulty making ourselves understood.

That analogy is less useful when we think that our hermeneutic may also be a kind of project, a work in progress, something that evolves and develops over time. This is an uncontroversial thing to say, since it is the basic premise of education. When others work on us and we work on ourselves in education, we are in the process of what Paulo Freire called 'conscientisation' or 'developing awareness'.

We can go through various kinds of hermeneutical conversions or paradigm shifts prompted by education, reflection or experience, all of which have a profound effect on how we read Scripture. This is a very common experience for ordinands, as they develop their critical engagement with texts – learning more about historical contexts, textual origins and developments –while also developing a greater awareness of critical theories of gender, culture and 'race'. It is also something that continues beyond university or college years and may have a major impact on how we read for preaching, even well into a long and established ministry. As Canadian singer Bruce Cockburn says, 'Sometimes a wind comes out of nowhere/And knocks you off your feet'.[3] I remember being stopped in my tracks by novelist and critic Marilynne Robinson's observation 'One of the things that has really struck me reading Calvin is what a strong sense he has that the aesthetic is the signature of the divine.'[4] Sometimes one comment, one line from a poem or

---

3 A line from Cockburn's song 'The Whole Night Sky' on the 1996 album *The Charity of Night*.

4 In a 2009 *Guardian* interview with Andrew Brown: www.theguardian.com/commentisfree/andrewbrown/2009/jun/04/religion-marilynne-robinson.

a song, one photograph or piece of art, can shift how we see the world and change our hermeneutic for ever.

That we are preachers who work with Scripture is likely (I hope!) to signal something about our approaching the Bible with a hermeneutic of trust, but as twenty-first-century readers we are also likely to approach Scripture with what Paul Ricoeur famously called 'a hermeneutic of suspicion'. This means that as readers, in Ricoeur's terms, we are driven by a 'double motivation: willingness to suspect, willingness to listen'.[5] Some forms of suspicion may be invited by the text, when devices such as irony and metaphor are deployed with the intent of encouraging us as readers to 'make more' of what is written and explore beneath the surface.[6] Other forms of suspicion may be brought to the text by us as critical readers, aware that we are interpreting ancient, pre-scientific texts, written in the context of patriarchy and religious or ideological struggles.

For preachers, then, this is about the work of awareness, realising we have a hermeneutic and seeking to be reflexive about what it is. It is also about awareness of work we need to do on our hermeneutic, as we seek to refine and develop it, drawing on knowledge and insight from many sides to help us understand more and better. This is not separate from the work of prayer, as we pray for divine illumination, but represents an affirmation of how the Spirit teaches us and leads us into truth.

One crucial way to characterise our hermeneutic is to think of it as our most basic assumptions about what 'the gospel' is. This is a key theme in the work of Canadian homiletics scholar Paul Scott Wilson,[7] and while it might seem a theological truism to say that preachers should proclaim the gospel, I often

---

5 Ricoeur (1970), p. 27.

6 On this see Christopher Bryan's chapter on 'The Hermeneutic of Suspicion', in Bryan and Landon (2013), pp. 24ff.

7 Author of many books including *The Practice of Preaching* (Wilson, 2007), and *Setting Words on Fire: Putting God at the Center of the Sermon* (Wilson, 2008).

find it a sobering reminder and a helpful check on my own practice. Which assumptions and motifs, which metaphors and messages, would other people hear most regularly in my preaching? How far would they hear them as good news?

In my own experience, there are some key statements about the gospel that I return to again and again when I am preparing to preach. One comes from Hans Küng, when he says: 'God's kingdom is creation healed.'[8] Another is John 10:10, where Jesus says, 'I came that they may have life and have it abundantly.' Another is from Revelation 21:5, where God says, 'See I am making all things new!' and from 2 Corinthians 5:19, 'In Christ, God was reconciling the world to himself.' Haunted by Wendell Berry's (Aristotelian/Thomistic) question 'What are people for?', like many in the Scottish reformed tradition, I return over and over to the claim in the Westminster Shorter Catechism that 'man's chief end is to glorify God and enjoy him for ever'.

I know this is simple stuff, but on days when I might lose my bearings as a believer and as a preacher this is true north for me. These are the bearings, the sightlines, the stars to steer by. Woe unto me if I do not preach a gospel of creation healed, of abundant life from Christ, of renewal and reconciliation in Christ. Woe to me if I do not preach this ecstatic anthropology: that we are made for God and made for joy.

To return to Newbigin, the sense in which he uses the term reminds us that our lives offer an ongoing interpretation of the gospel, both as individuals and as congregations. We not only have a hermeneutic, we are a hermeneutic for others. Preachers' lives interpret their sermons, and the culture and practice of congregations interprets what is preached within them; this is, to be sure, a sobering, shaming and challenging thought, but it may also, on reflection, prove to be a gracious and reassuring one for preachers.

---

8 Küng (1977), p. 231.

# 2.5 Converging literacies

Reading for a sermon is an intentional process and it can even be an anxious one. I am reading this text in order to preach and to some extent I am reading it 'on behalf of' those I will preach to; will I find and see things in it that will 'preach'? In this practice of reading *towards* the sermon, a number of literacies need to come together, to converge and fuse in a process of understanding. There is a literary-critical capacity to read the scriptural text, a social-political capacity to read 'the world' in front of the text, a theological capacity to read the text in light of our knowledge of God, and a missional-pastoral capacity to read and relate to the lives of those we preach to.

These are never fully realised capacities and none of us are equally capable or proficient in all of them, although the way some preachers combine them leaves me awestruck. There is also, as we have noted all through this book, a necessary confession to be made whenever we talk about ability, capacity or skill as if it were something that could be freestanding, apart from the choice of God and the work of the Holy Spirit. This confession might be all the more important the more 'proficient' we become as preachers, because we may become able to deliver something that appears to be a virtuoso performance, but are actually 'phoning' it in.

We should always aim to remember that reading for preaching is something that is spiritually provisional, which has a certain tentativeness to it, which is open to the enlightening action of God. That said, these are real literacies, not ones that are 'magically' or miraculously acquired. We need a theology of creation and of regeneration (and I find Barth a compelling example of this) that, in the words of Psalm 90:17, prays for God to 'establish the work of our hands'. The practice of reading we aim at is a practice in which both this divine establishing and this human work are fully embraced.

So long as we go on preaching, we are working to become more literate, to develop our capacity to read text, world and congregation. We work on these distinct literacies at different times and in different ways, so that they can be offered to God as we read towards the sermon. (Equally, if we neglect any of them, we may limit and reduce our own capacity to minister.)

When they converge powerfully in the process of reading, we may often not be self-conscious of how this convergence is happening, because we are caught up in a disclosive process in which we are finding meaning, making meaning, seeing and making connections. To take up an appropriate Biblical-theological metaphor, we may experience this as a kind of inspiration, or insight; there may at times be a sense of givenness to it. Certainly, if we have a holistic theology of how God establishes us in our understanding, that sets us up to receive all insight and understanding as gift, while not underestimating the extent to which the prophetic insight that we recognise in a sermon preached to us is the result of hard study, attentive listening, open and receptive cultural and personal encounter, patient reflection, and an exhausting, immersive experience of struggle and service. That brilliant illustration from a recent film is there because the preacher takes the time (a) to go to the cinema, and (b) to read, think and talk about films. That powerful connection to economic policy is there because the preacher takes time to read and view current affairs coverage. That alignment between the poetics of the text and the poetics of the sermon is there because the preacher worked hard to understand the poetics of the text. That awareness of the potential depths of human experience implicit within a textual detail is there because the preacher is drawing on personal empathy and pastoral experience. That sense of how people from different classes, cultures, ethnicities or genders might 'hear' something in the text is there because the preacher is drawing on reserves of critical, cultural understanding, built up through experience, dialogue and reading.

For many of us, if we have been through university or seminary, developing these capacities will involve extensive study and high levels of academic literacy and engagement, but there is no intrinsic need for this to be so. These kinds of literacy could be powerfully present in someone with little academic training or formal education, and painfully lacking in someone with multiple degrees.

When we read towards a sermon, these literacies converge in an encounter with the specific 'resistance' of any given text and with the nexus of literary, political, theological and pastoral issues that face us in confronting 'this text'.

# 2.6 Cues for the sermon

Reading towards a sermon begins for me as a more open process, a wondering about what will emerge, which involves a number of 'passes' through the texts set for the day. The reading is already 'cued' by the contexts, political, historical, congregational and personal, that make us as preachers liable to notice and to fix on certain ideas, details and features of the text. One of the peculiar delights and regular surprises of being reunited with a text, even one we think we know well, can be the experience of noticing something, of being caught by something that we have never seen before. The opposite and less encouraging experience is when we only seem to read 'the same' in it as before and start to wonder (even sometimes to panic) if we have anything new to say this time around ...

In these moments, the act of reading shows itself as a process of making meaning, of construing sense, of thinking 'how to take' a word or phrase and what to make of it. There can be a pressure that comes with this, even an anxiety. Anxious reading brings with it a feeling of being stuck, confounded – as if we have stopped in a forest or a desert to read a map and are unsure which direction to strike out in. In my experience, anxious reading moves too fast and misses things. The remedy is almost always to slow down and to force oneself back into a 'close reading' of the text. It may involve a stopping to pray; or the slowing down, breathing and refocusing may itself feel like a form of prayer.

Finding my cues in the text is usually about finding somewhere to begin, which in the end may or may not turn out to be what the sermon begins with. It's about fixing on, or being hooked in by something, in the text – more than that, it's about beginning to 'hear' something in the text, which sounds, even if very faintly, like it could be God speaking. Here we have to do with the spiritual discipline or dance of reading for preaching. It can be maddeningly, infuriatingly and even terrifyingly unpredictable in its timing. Sometimes I feel as though I hear and know the cue for a sermon within seconds, while other times it takes hours or days. When it takes longer, the 'reading' continues inside us as preachers while swimming, running or walking the dog; maybe even while falling asleep or waking up.

There has to be an honourable mention here for all of the resources that help us to read, the scholars and thinkers we read along with, as we are preparing. The cue is often found in a commentary, which redirects my thoughts about a passage, reminding or informing me of a key detail or prompting me to read from a new angle. It may come from theology as much as from Biblical studies, when I realise that the reason I am struggling to construe something is because I can't get the theological grammar into shape in my head, so that I take down a volume to read about the doctrine that is at stake, rather than read a specific reflection on particular verses.

The process of finding a 'cue' marks the hinge between reading and speaking, between discovery and production, between hearing God speak to me and sharing what I have heard with others. A lot turns on it, perhaps the whole sermon. It's what gets things moving.

## 2.7 Working the verbs

### Learning from Anna Carter Florence

In 2012, homiletics professor Anna Carter Florence graciously came to Glasgow from Atlanta, Georgia, to give the Mair Lectures and to lead a workshop on preaching for our students. The workshop was a particularly memorable experience, led by Anna with the combination of insight, and the intensity (the good kind!) that is part of her singular gifting. We sat in a circle of about twenty students, a mix of Presbyterians and Baptists; she gave us the text to read in pairs or triplets, and then we began to work on it ourselves. What came next was a remarkable master class in group hermeneutics, organised around the discipline of 'working the verbs' in the passage. As someone who tries to be a teacher, it was a joy to watch such a gifted colleague take the group on a journey of dialogue, questioning, co-operation, and the sharing of insights. At times there was an intensity to the experience that made it feel like a group therapy session, as we worked with the gospel passage, a healing narrative. As we worked the verbs, patiently, one by one, one after another, in a communal close reading, Anna would stop with individuals, sometimes half kneeling in front of them, coaxing them and cajoling them to 'read' the verb in question. There was laughter and disclosure, puzzlement, resistance, disquiet, emotion, a chewing on the words, some questions about the Greek, and the strange spiritual alchemy in which we began to hear notes and nuances in the text. She was teaching us to read. For preaching.

In particular, she was teaching us to read verbs, to think about a particular set of dynamics in the text, about who was *doing* what, about what was *happening*, about active and passive voices, and she was doing the classic close reading work of slowing us down, making us pay attention, and making us become aware. Like many great moments of teaching and learning, it was very simple – but also complex and fruitful.

So when we read for preaching, we need to work the verbs.

# 2.8 Working the nouns

The Baptist homiletician Stuart Blythe was sitting in on Anna's 'verbs' workshop with some of his students, and as we compared appreciative notes afterwards he made a balancing point about the importance of nouns. If I caught his meaning rightly, it was a reminder of the importance of reading for what is fixed alongside what is fluid. When we read for preaching, we read to 'take' an idea or thought from the text into the sermon, to convert it from its original use to a new and contemporary use. That is intrinsic to what preaching is. Previously I spoke about the specific resistance of a text and how this acts as a force or better interacts with the meaning-making, construing work of the reader. I am generalising here, but if verbs belong more to the 'convertible' and malleable nature of a text, nouns (particularly proper nouns) can be associated with what moors a text in context and, in so doing, charges it with that resistance. We are talking about the 'suffered under Pontius Pilate' aspect of a text, which we could shorthand as 'historical' – although historical writing has its own strongly liquid and constructive tendencies.

This is also part of what keeps the text at a distance from us. The danger with verbs is that we might keep assimilating the text, making it familiar, assigning it an ancillary role in illustrating some dimension of 'the sacred'. Nouns are part of what keeps it strange, keeps it old, keeps it Jewish, keeps it other. The long names our readers stumble over in church interfere with our domesticating a text and our taking it over. They pose awkward questions to our strategies of demythologising. As we read for preaching, this turns out to be profoundly important, because it reminds us that we may need these spaces between another time and our time, another place and our place, another culture and our culture. These spaces may be critically important spaces, where we have to be self-conscious (and suspicious) about the hermeneutical operations we are performing and cannot just read over what was 'God's will' then, to what God requires of us now, or how the world seemed then, to how we see it now.

I have played with this opposition between verb and noun to make a point, and although I think it works as an illustration, I don't advocate holding it too tightly or forensically. The point will need to be worked out differently in different passages and will blur the actual verb/noun distinctions in some of them.

On a less playful note, this brief technical exercise of focusing on nouns is also another very basic technique within close reading, which slows us down and makes us attend to what is on the page.

# 2.9 Losing control – knots in the text

## Learning from Stephen D. Moore

Back in the days that we might call 'peak-Derrida', the late 1980s and early 1990s, another book that was formative in teaching me to read was Stephen Moore's radical and remarkable 1989 book, *Literary Criticism and the Gospels*. It was a provocative challenge to my view of the Biblical text, with its unsettling vision of 'stories of reading that have no ending'. That phrase has resonated with my experience of preaching ever since. Every three years, a text appears in the lectionary asking – sometimes daring and defying us – to read it again, not least when there is an initial dissonance between text and context or occasion. Looking back over three decades, the late 1980s and early 1990s marked the ascendancy of a literary-critical paradigm over a historical-critical one in Biblical studies, accompanied by significant amounts of rhetoric, now much less common, about the rise of 'the postmodern Bible'. Back then, Stephen Moore commented 'as the challenge was once to come to terms with the modernist bible, so now the challenge is to come to terms with its postmodern successor'.[1]

We hear less of that rhetoric in the worlds of academic theology and Biblical studies today, but like many others of a certain age I was changed by 'postmodernism' and in particu-

---

1 Moore (1989), pp. 129–30; also quoted in Goldingay (1993).

lar it changed me as a reader. In an earlier section I talked about the experience of moving on from an anxiously protective stance towards Scripture, something that I came to realise had practical hermeneutical consequences.

Moore's book, in which I also found much with which to differ, contains a memorable section entitled 'Stories of Reading that Come Undone'. His contribution here to the phenomenology of reading takes in the experience of encountering 'knots' in the text. Leonard Cohen famously sang to his lover that they should not talk of 'love or chains, or things we can't untie'.[2] Moore offers an account of hermeneutical experience in which the knots in the text that we can't untie cause the act of reading itself to 'come undone'. Specifically, what he suggests comes undone is our experience of reading as 'mastery' of the text, as a process that we are in control of and where all is proceeding as we expect it to.[3] For Moore, this experience of losing control of the reading process has the potential to be a moment of hermeneutical clarity, when we are freed to see and say more about how we were trying to read, what we were trying to do to the text, what we are afraid of if the knot remains stubbornly tight, and what the consequences will be if we find a text to be somehow unreadable.[4]

Moore's instincts in *Literary Criticism and the Gospels* are radically deconstructive and I would not want his to be the only books on my preaching bookshelf, but I have found this insight to be a liberating one for me. As a preacher, there is a lot of felt pressure to explain the text, to solve textual problems and share solutions with the congregation, to crack the

---

2 From 'Hey That's No Way To Say Goodbye', *Songs of Leonard Cohen*, 1967 (some versions have the thing we can't untie as change, others as chains ...).

3 See the header quotes from David Fisher, 'The Phenomenology of Displacement' and John Caputo 'Radical Hermeneutics', at the beginning of chapter 8, p. 131 (Moore, 1989).

4 One of my teachers in Biblical studies, the late Bob Carroll, wrote a book on the Bible called *Wolf in the Sheepfold* (Carroll, 1991).

code and decipher what is mysterious. We feel ourselves, like scriptural spin doctors, to be charged with protecting the reputation of the Bible and, in the reformed tradition, the principle of *claritas scripturae* brings its own pressure to bear. (Alister McGrath has commented that the exegetical optimism of the reformers that this doctrine expressed foundered on the inability of the reformers to agree on their doctrine of communion![5])

Without pushing my own practice to the outer limits that Moore plays at, the idea that knots and tangles in the text – the points that exert the most stubborn resistance to my eagerness to resolve and explain, that these might be points of disclosure and grace – has been of great practical help to me. For one thing, they promote humility, as we preachers step back from our easy assumptions that we are in control of a text and are forced to ask what we were trying to do. They also challenge us as preachers in terms of what we will go on to say about these texts that may have vexed and troubled us. I will come back to that in Part 3. They keep us reading and keep us aware that we never truly 'finish a book', particularly the Bible. Finally, they too send us back to prayer, to a hermeneutics of trust, to a theology of canon, and to a remembering that we are part of a community of readers and interpreters. Within this, the work of the Holy Spirit, whose fruit is patience, may sometimes be to help us to wait with the 'things we can't untie'.

5 McGrath (2012), p. 107.

# 2.10 Preach like Jacob

A later section will take its cue from a bishop urging us not to be like Jacob, but here, and not with great originality, I am looking to the famous story in Genesis 32 in which Jacob wrestles with God. It is a narrative of extraordinary depth and power, one that we are never done with reading. It also works, in my experience, as one of the most powerful metaphors for the process of reading for preaching.[1]

In conversations with students both inside and outside class, who are in the early days of their preaching ministry, I often hear evidence of how they 'freeze' in front of a passage, when it seems to read 'blank' to them, when they are finding no cues, no points of entry or points of departure. Under pressure to produce a sermon, they may fashion something that has only a tangential relationship to the Bible readings. In the imagery of Genesis 32, they let go too soon, they release their grip on the passage, stop reading, and go off to seek the blessing elsewhere.

Not all experiences of reading for preaching end equally well. Each year in preaching class, we laugh together with relief at Chris Erdman's sage advice: 'If your sermon's a dog, walk it proudly.'[2] So my resort to Genesis 32 is not meant to suggest that all reading for preaching ends with the blessing of all the

---

1 In Gauguin's painting *After the Sermon* referred to earlier, it is this scene from Genesis that the worshippers continue to see 'in their mind's eye'.

2 Erdman (2007), p. 175.

insight we need. It is meant to encourage other preachers, as it encourages me, to remember that reading in preparation for preaching may be a rough business, a spiritual struggle, a hermeneutical wrestling match.[3] To read like Jacob is to 'wrestle and fight and pray', to believe that the one we wrestle with is able to bless us and to hold on as long and tenaciously as we can, in the hope that things will end well.

---

3 In which the text may even 'fight dirty' and wound us, leave us limping away as the sun comes up.

# PART 3

# Speaking

# 3.1 Beginnings and endings

Sermons have to start and end somewhere and somehow. Finding how to do this is always tricky. Exposition, when it is based on running commentary, may seem to suggest that, in the spirit of Rodgers and Hammerstein, we simply start at the very beginning and that this is a very good place to start. Even then, our first words are likely to be scene setting, a way of staging and approaching the text.

Walter Brueggemann suggests that when they are preaching, 'the pastors of the church must make an outrageous act of subversive rationality' and identifies long sermon introductions with the opposite of this, seeing them as designed to reassure the congregation that what follows will fit in with their existing mindset. He cites Karl Barth's sermons as a better example: 'He just starts: and the very first sentence he utters calls the whole world into question.'[1]

This is at least an interesting way to think about beginnings, although it does set the bar high. Roger Bowen, who quotes this, adds his own advice about not starting with jokes, or apologies, or being too obvious and boring.[2] I don't violently disagree with that, but I have never felt comfortable with the idea that there were rules or formulas. Bowen stresses the need to 'arouse the interest' of the congregation, in case they decide

---

1 From a 1987 lecture to students in Nottingham, quoted in Bowen (2005), p. 29.
2 Ibid., pp. 28–9.

immediately to go to sleep; again, there is something to that, but I can also imagine feeling that someone was trying too hard to hook me in. I know that sometimes, depending on the shape of what is coming, I start in very ordinary and natural-istic terms, while at other times I opt for something more striking and stylised.

Some forms of the new hermeneutic used to insist that preachers had to establish a vivid 'inductive' connection to the culture and experience of the congregation as part of the opening 'move' of the sermon. Again, that can be effective, but there might be other ways to build a connection more slowly. The length of the sermon may also have a bearing on its shape, on how it begins, and on what can be sustained. There are no hard-and-fast rules, but:

- I always try to be particularly aware of the beginning and ending, so that I don't, by accident or carelessness, stumble into a rambling beginning or bring things to an abrupt end.
- Both beginnings and endings should be related to what the sermon is *doing*, and I always find it helpful to think about how they relate to one another, how they 'frame' the sermon.
- The ending of a sermon should be crafted with an awareness of what is coming next within the liturgy and vice versa, noting that this should sometimes be silence.

# 3.2  Don't preach like Jacob

## Learning from Miles Davis

'Sometimes you have to play a long time to play like yourself.'

There are different versions of this in circulation, so Miles Davis
may have said it more than once. Another is 'it takes a lot of
practice to sound like yourself'. Whichever are the *ipsissima
verba*, for many of us when we hear it there are rueful smiles
and nods of recognition. There are many varied journeys to
finding our voices as preachers, and perhaps some people feel
from the outset that they just *do* sound like themselves. For
others, and I count myself among them, that is a much harder
place to reach. In both the Church of England and the Church
of Scotland when I was a student, prominent preachers created speaking styles that their admirers and mentees adopted.
A generation of Anglican preachers came to sound like John
Stott and a generation of Presbyterian preachers to sound like
Willie Still or Eric Alexander. Perhaps today, hipster preachers
aspire to sound like Rob Bell and alpha male preachers like
Mark Driscoll?

An obvious issue with all these examples is that they are all
men. The rapid growth in the number of women preachers
since the 1960s has helped to break the mould here, though
only because for many of them there was initially at least, no
mould to follow. This tendency to ape, copy or align is not
something to be despised, because it reveals something basic

about how any of us learn. We learn by copying, imitating and mimicking, whether we are jazz musicians or preachers. We are inducted into a craft tradition, and that is just how we learn and grow as human beings. Such traditions will seem to be in bad order when it begins to feel as if they produce clones and soundalikes, who lack authenticity and personality. Preaching is personal communication, and it can only be done in our own bodies, in our own voices. We find ourselves in trouble when our preaching voice sounds wrong to ourselves, when we are dissociating, coming apart, separating self from voice.

This is where the counsel comes to *not* be like Jacob, from the wise Ugandan bishop Festo Kivengere, who said to preachers: 'Don't be like Jacob, pretending to be someone else in order to get the blessing!'[1] I love this quote and it sits alongside the Miles Davis quote as an encouragement to us as preachers to find our voices. The journey to finding our own preaching voices can be a tortuous one and may prove to be a therapeutic one, involving many of the demands and struggles that therapy requires of us. There are, I think, a few key principles:

- **God wills and loves difference**
  We don't all have to sound the same. Our accent, whether it is from Aberdeen or Cardiff, Alabama or Lagos, is the right accent to preach in.

- **Different voices make different things easy or hard to say, or to hear**
  The strong, ringing, sharp voice will work for some things, but the soft, high or delicate voice will work for others. Most of us don't have completely versatile and all-purpose voices.

---

1 Quoted in Bowen (2005), p. 32.

- **Voices come with bodies attached**
  Female voices can say some things with authority that male voices cannot. Black voices can bear witness to things that white voices cannot. Sometimes, as in the funeral sermon included earlier, we may 'borrow' authority by quoting from someone who has an authority we lack.[2]

- **Practice can help**
  Reflective practice means we can work on our voices; we can set out to *find* our voices. A growth in confidence, assertiveness, humility or empathy may change our voices in ways that are a blessing to us and to others. That will often lead to a real, acoustic, tonal change in how we 'sound', but it may also involve a change of pathos and ethos, which impacts on how we hear ourselves and others hear us. Voice workshops or acting workshops can teach us to use our voice as an instrument and explore its expressive possibilities.[3]

- **We're not all Morgan Freeman or Maggie Smith**
  Finding our voices doesn't mean we will all be able to do the same things with them, even after a lot of work. Preaching is a performative practice and different preachers can take the poetics of performance to different places and different levels.

The desire to sound like ourselves, and the journey we take in practice towards feeling that we do sound like ourselves, involve preachers in profound personal-spiritual moves towards valuing our own bodies and learning to be our redeemed selves in Christ. I say personal-spiritual, but it also needs to be emphasised that such moves are political and cultural. This is

---

2 I owe this insight about 'borrowing' authority to Ron Rienstra; obviously the borrowing should be attributed and respectful – it should also be aware of the possibility that it may become inappropriate 'appropriation': using someone else to make us look good!

3 Mennonite homiletician Allan Rudy Froese sings the praises of the veteran voice coach Kirstin Linklater www.linklatervoice.com.

particularly important when we are unlearning, resisting and rewriting cultural scripts or overturning patterns of historical dominance, which have worked to devalue our bodies and silence our voices. This is a journey of lifelong learning and discipleship, which never ends until 'we know fully, even as we have been fully known' (1 Cor. 13:12).

# 3.3 Writing for the ear

It is a staple of classes in preaching, as also of classes or courses in speechwriting, scriptwriting and playwriting, that you need to learn to write for the ear not the eye. The most common problem with student sermons is that at least in parts they can sound like someone is reading aloud from an essay. The basic insight is that when we see writing, our eyes can return to recap, reread, review, but when we hear speech, our ears, hearts and minds have one chance to catch and hold it. Speech vanishes with time, unless memory holds on to it for us.

Lutheran Professor of Rhetoric Gracia Grindal captures helpfully the change brought about by the rise of print culture, as writing for the eye led to the production of a plainer style, less encumbered by the conventions of classical rhetoric.[1] Having learned to write that way, the challenge for those beginning to preach is to learn new ways to write, to produce sermon scripts that can be turned into moving and memorable speech. Since this is primarily a reflective book rather than a 'how-to' book, I am not going to list the techniques that might help with this. It is also important to remember that these vary across cultures. Preachers formed in certain church cultures are often deeply attuned to the kind of oral performance that will communicate and resonate with their congregations. In church cultures that lack clear or unified traditions and conventions of oral

---

1 Gracia Grindal's brief 2010 article on 'Writing for the Ear' can be viewed at www.workingpreacher.org/craft.aspx?m=4377&post=1710; see also Jacks (1981).

performance, we will have to work at the skills and techniques that help us to speak and others to listen.[2]

The key thing is that we get the point and we do something about it. If our sermons only work in print, we're not doing it right.

---

2 This is an area where congregational feedback could be very important, see section 4.10 on p. 141.

# 3.4  How literary form informs the sermon

I have already mentioned how important Thomas Long's work on literary forms has been for me and I want to return to it here. Long comments:

> It is ironic that preachers often disregard these dimensions of a text since attention to these 'textual poetics' brings us into contact with what resonates most harmoniously with a key ingredient in the homiletical task: deciding how to preach so that the sermon embodies in its language, form and style the gospel it seeks to proclaim.[1]

Long recognised that putting this relatively simple idea to work required a relatively complex process. It involved combining an attentiveness to literary features of the text with an understanding of related rhetorical dynamics:

> Literary features are in the text, rhetorical dynamics, though caused by the text, are in the reader.
>
> Much of the time, however, genres have more complex and multi-layered rhetorical functions. It is not easy to say what a parable or a psalm or a proverb is likely to do for and to a reader, and any attempt to describe the rhetorical dynamics of such genres will be found wanting. Nevertheless, each genre does possess specific rhetorical impact.[2]

---

1 Long (1989), p. 12.
2 Ibid., p. 26.

Long suggests a sequence of genre questions, text questions and homiletical questions to help the preacher move from a more general attention to the literary and rhetorical dimensions of genre, to the specific sense of how a particular text was operating within that genre, and finally to how a sermon on that text might be influenced by understanding it as a particular example of the genre.[3]

Long was careful to warn preachers that he was not advocating any simple attempt at replicating the genre of the text in the genre of the sermon. It might, he said, offer a model in some instances, but often the sermonic form will be 'markedly different'.[4]

Long's work had such a strong impact on me, some two decades ago, just because I realised that most sermons I had ever heard showed very little, if any, sign of having been shaped by the genre of Biblical literature they were 'about'. That remains true of most sermons I have heard since then. Not only that, while hearing his warning about not trying to directly map one form on to another, I had and have a troubling sense that many sermons did the opposite – they effectively cancelled out the genre of the text they were working with. There is a homiletic equivalent of Vanhoozer's hermeneutical flattening, in which the genre of sermon is so unexamined, undifferentiated and unintentional that it simply, in Thomas Long's already quoted image, throws the text into some kind of juicer to squeeze out the ideas and then works out how to preach them.[5]

I don't want to overclaim for my own practice here. I have found – and still find – Long's orientation to preachers here to be challenging and even overwhelming; but I also find it continually stimulating and provocative, even if it is sometimes hard for preachers to metabolise. The truth is that for most of

---

3 Ibid., p. 24.
4 Ibid., pp. 33–4.
5 Ibid., pp. 11–12.

us, in our preaching situations and contexts, 'sermon' is a kind of genre in itself. It is a genre constituted by our own voice, by our liturgical context and congregational expectations, by our own preaching habits, and by the range of pastoral things we are trying to attend to while preaching. A thoroughgoing appropriation of Long's points, even though they now seem obvious and unavoidable to me, would push me towards a more radical and experimental poetics of preaching than I often feel I have the courage, imagination and permission to attempt!

The literary turn in Biblical studies and hermeneutics has decisively changed the way I read, but decades later it is still working on how I speak as a preacher. I am, however, surrounded by its questions, which work on me as I work on a sermon: What kind of literature is this? What conventions and expectations does this genre bring with it and how might they shape sermonic form? How should the textual poetics feed the poetics of the sermon? What about mood and tone? What about the function of language within this reading? What is being commended or forbidden? Who says and why? What kind of poetry is this? How do I read this law? How should the language of the sermon track, replicate, challenge or disavow the language of the text?

These questions drive us towards another set of questions about the different sub-genres that we can develop within the overall genre of sermon. When does the literary form shape the sermonic form as well as its content – what it does as well as what it is about – and how far can/should we take this? For my part, in two of my bolder preaching moments, the response to these questions was to ignore Long's advice and try to align literary form and sermonic form more closely.

This first sermon was preached at a service of infant baptism and communion in a multicultural inner-city church in East London, on the Sunday before Lent. Although it was not the densest or thickest of textual knots, I had long struggled with how to 'read' and understand the English word 'blessed' in the Beatitudes.[6] Moore's by then tried and tested advice to pay particular attention to these moments when you 'fail' as a reader, combined with Long's work, led me to this sermon. In it, I use the rhetorical form of pronouncing blessings to work out my struggle to read and understand the literary form of a beatitude. By practising blessings, and making the sermon solely out of and into blessings, I try to read and perform their reality. There was no introduction, it simply began out of a silence after the Gospel reading:

Blessed are those who don't think they know it all
Blessed are those who know they don't have it all
Blessed are those who know they have fallen short
Blessed are those who feel their own unworthiness
Blessed are those who know their need of God
Blessed are those who trust in God's grace to help them
Blessed are those who trust in God's Son to save them,
Blessed are babies who are baptised without any say in it
*Blessed are the poor in spirit, for theirs is the kingdom of heaven.*

Blessed are those whose hearts are not made of stone
Blessed are those who know how to cry
Blessed are those who love so much it hurts
Blessed are those who know the world deserves better
Blessed are those who have some regrets
Blessed are those who drive themselves to tears
Blessed are those who want life after death
Blessed are those who weep at the grave of Lazarus
Blessed are babies who cry when they need to
*Blessed are those who mourn, for they shall be comforted.*

---

6 I mean by this the ongoing struggle to get inside a word/concept even after the initial technical, translation work and a good deal of reading commentaries on the text.

Blessed are those who don't drive in the bus lanes
Blessed are all cyclists
Blessed are those who know how to queue
Blessed are those who know when they have enough
Blessed are those who don't think size matters
Blessed are those who need others
Blessed are those who are good listeners
Blessed are those not so full of themselves they don't have
    room for others
Blessed are babies who let you dress them in any colour
    combination
*Blessed are the meek, for they shall inherit the earth.*

Blessed are those who ask what's goin' on
Blessed are those who rage against the machine
Blessed are those who stand up to the bosses
Blessed are those who pay their union dues
Blessed are those who vote for tax rises
Blessed are those who fight racism
Blessed are those who shop in the E5 shop[7]
Blessed are those who give to Christian Aid
Blessed are those who vote
Blessed are those who demonstrate
Blessed are those who want the world turned upside down
Blessed are babies who yell when they're hungry and thirsty,
*Blessed are those who hunger and thirst for righteousness,*
    *for they will be filled.*

Blessed are those who forgive us
Blessed are those who give us another chance
Blessed are those who take us back …
Blessed are those who put up with us
Blessed are those who love people more than rules
Blessed are babies who grow up OK despite our mistakes
*Blessed are the merciful, they will receive mercy.*

---

7 Our local church-sponsored social enterprise.

Blessed are those who know they can't have it all
Blessed are those who have a sense of direction
Blessed are those who don't cheat on their lovers
Blessed are those who want others to do well
Blessed are those who love themselves
Blessed are those who emancipate themselves from
    mental slavery
Blessed are those who mean it
Blessed are babies who love us because we are their parents
*Blessed are the pure in heart, for they shall see God.*

Blessed are those who don't stir it
Blessed are those who don't love their neighbour's flag less
    than their own
Blessed are those who try to stop tanks with their bare hands
Blessed are those who take time to understand
Blessed are those who get shot at by both sides
Blessed are those who compromise
Blessed are babies who can do no violence to anyone
*Blessed are the peacemakers, for they will be called children*
    *of God*

Blessed are those who get roughed up because they dared to
    get involved
Blessed are those who dictators try to silence
Blessed are those who don't take bribes
Blessed are those who don't compromise ...
Blessed are babies when they show us the true value of life
*Blessed are those who are persecuted for righteousness' sake*

Blessed are those who stand up for Jesus
Blessed are those who wear the ash on their heads all
    through Wednesday
Blessed are those who share the gospel
Blessed are babies who are signed with the sign of the cross
*Rejoice and be glad – for their reward is great in heaven.*

*They are a fresh prophecy from the God of Life, the God of Jesus Christ.*

Blessed are you who have seen these babies baptised today
This is grace for you also,
Blessed are you who come to the Lord's Table to share
 bread and wine
Jesus Christ is here for you, in the power of the Holy Spirit,
 to meet you and to bless you.
Glory to God, the source of all blessing, now and forever,
 Amen.

I include this sermon not because it is typical of how this challenge should be worked out, but because it was helpful for me on this particular occasion to push the genre further than I had before. Although it remains a more experimental use of form for me, it confirmed my sense of how important it was to be influenced by the form of the passage. Some genres will translate more easily than others and some, like this one, may translate more directly than others. Another key thing for me here was that the use of form acted as a kind of hermeneutical 'probe', helping me to explore meaning, effect and affect, where I was struggling to read and 'hear' the Gospel text and to 'open' it to others.[8]

The second sermon, on Jeremiah 28, was preached to a small group of staff and students at Trinity College worship, in the University of Glasgow Chapel.

To all the exiles:
Thus says the LORD, the God of Israel
I have sent you into exile in Babylon

---

8 Of course there is significant anachronism here, but the point still holds. I am not claiming to have replicated or recreated a rhetorical situation from first-century Palestine so much as to have explored some of my own mental images about what that was; images and assumptions that were already shaping and controlling my reading of this passage from the Sermon on the Mount.

You are going nowhere quickly,
Don't let the Ba-bylonians grind you down!

Build
Live
Plant
Love

Marry
Multiply
Grow
Pray

Build houses – build them strong – take your time – dig foundations – build them to last – build extra bedrooms for the kids and for their kids.
Build houses to last you seventy years – and live in them – unpack the suitcases then throw them away – put your pictures up – make the place homely.
And outside mark the plots where you will bury both the elders and yourselves – you're going nowhere quickly.

You must live here – I mean you to live – within these walls, in the secret spaces, behind closed doors, prayers can be said and secrets whispered, the songs of Zion can be sung, the language kept alive, the stories told, your children taught, within these walls – dreams can be kept alive – the dreams that Babylon cannot control.

To all the exiles:
Plant gardens, take your time and build raised beds, dig ditches to water them, plan your crop rotations,
plant trees that will take decades to give you fruit
the earth will keep on giving to you – dig the soil, push the seed in the ground, cover and water it, fertilise the crops, wait for the sun and the rain – plant olives and vines, plant figs

and pomegranates, plant lemons and oranges, almonds and
apples – bend your tastes to foreign food.
Plant wheat for bread and vines for wine – this is your Eden
– this is your Canaan – this is your shift – this is your time –
this is your place.
Here you must plant and harvest and eat and share – you are
going nowhere quickly.
Within these gardens, seeds can grow, seeds of resistance and
renewal, seeds of change, seeds of the future, seeds of hope.
Under these trees when they are grown, your children will sit
down in circles
and will plan the journey home.

To all the exiles:
Don't let the empire make you hate yourselves. Fall in love
with one another – take wives and husbands – give yourselves
to one another – dance at each other's weddings – make new
families, you are going nowhere quickly.
Make love, make babies,
Be proud when your bellies stretch and swell, they are full of
the promise of your future,
welcome and bless your sons and daughters,
teach them the old stories in new ways
Multiply, multiply, multiply – become more
don't let Babylon reduce you, make you less,
grow up and on into the people you were made and meant
to be.

To all the exiles:
Take this place of cursing, cruelty, enslavement
take this place of exile, this non-home,
these enemies and masters, bullies, racists, bosses
take them and seek their welfare – you are going nowhere
quickly.

Bring your best to their worst –
dig tunnels of hope under the foundations of empire
pray hard for Babylon, pray daily for its good, seek its shalom,
in its shalom your own is lodged for now
do good, show love, do justice, live in peace –
create a colony of heaven
that the power of empire cannot overcome.

To all the exiles:
I know the plans I have for you
Plans for your good, not for your harm
To give you all a future and a hope
I will restore you, I will gather you and bring you back,
I will be found by you and hear you –
you are going nowhere quickly.

Build – Live – Plant – Harvest – Love – Marry – Multiply –
Grow – Pray – Love – Hope
Seek the welfare of the city. For in it you will find your own.
Amen.[9]

---

9 If you detect the influence of Walter Brueggemann behind this reading of
Jeremiah, you are not wrong.

# 3.5 Preaching without a script

Every year in our introductory preaching classes someone will follow my lead and preach with a script and it just feels wrong, as if they are tongue-tied, weighed down and unnatural. So we go on to explore the question: maybe you're not a script preacher? I grew up in the kind of fundamentalist church where no one would dare to have a script and even notes were frowned upon, as a sign of the preacher being 'unspiritual'.[1] Sadly, most of the preaching was terrible, but as time went on I encountered many scriptless preachers whose sermons were wonderful.

I rarely preach without a script. I find it very challenging – verging on terrifying – and I also find that the poetics of my preaching style require the writing stage for me to fix them, while recognising that I always need to try to write for the ear. I should probably dare myself to do it more often. For some people, scriptless preaching is what they are made and meant to do. Obviously, this is not the same as preaching without preparation and most scriptless preachers have notes, or use projected slides to cue them. Responding more freely to a structure created by slides with a mix of bullet points, quotes and visual images is the closest I usually get to scriptless preaching and, at times, I do get a whiff of the intoxicating freedom of those preachers who 'walk on water'.

---

1 See Bryan D. Spinks in Vischer, ed. (2003), pp. 66–84; and Alan P. Sell in Vischer, ed. (2003), pp. 83–106, for discussion of theological and spiritual privileging of the extempore and unwritten in worship.

I have very little wisdom to offer on this subject – better to look to those who are more expert practitioners. I can only offer encouragement to those who find scripts inhibit and weigh them down to take the time and practice to discover if their default preaching approach should be to step out of the boat and work without one.

# 3.6 Preaching with a script

We might seem to have already covered this in the section on writing for the ear, but I want to think more positively about the possibilities of preaching *with* a script. An emphasis on poetics, both in literary terms and in preaching, has been a running theme of this book and I want to reflect on how that shapes the practice of preaching. The poetics of oral communication do not depend upon a script, but a script allows them to be shaped and prepared in advance.

An emphasis on poetics and performance in preaching has not always been welcomed. Karl Barth was famously unkeen on rhetoric and, more commonly, within the Church language about performance is easily misunderstood, sometimes getting sucked into conservative rants about worship not being entertainment.

To speak about the performative element in preaching is to lay stress on the way in which *form performs content* and is not just a container for 'ideational matter'. That we receive the word through a full spectrum performance of it belongs to a properly understood doctrine of creation, embodiment and incarnation.

When the Scriptures are translated, translators attempt to render the poetry and the imagery of the Hebrew or Greek texts in the English text. When we read Biblical poetry, whether erotic or prophetic, when we read a psalm or a parable, when we read apocalyptic, the words cannot simply be reduced to ideas or propositions. Just as the words of Scripture *perform* the beauty or terror, the lament or celebration, so the words of a sermon do also.

The script allows the preacher to offer to God and the congregation a considered, crafted and chosen word – whether it is John Stott's three perfectly poised points beginning with P or the lush, daring lyricism of my Glasgow colleague Heather Walton, the feminist theologian, poetics scholar and preacher.

To offer you four points beginning with P, since they began to trip out accidentally in this script, a script can have a *protective* and *pastoral* function, because it allows us to think before we speak when tackling delicate and controversial issues. It has a *practical* function, because it helps us to remember and time what we want to say. It has a *poetic* function, because it allows us to pre-craft the language for oral delivery.

The other P that merits a mention here is pretentiousness or preciousness. An overemphasis on the poetics of our preaching might lead us to become self-indulgent and mannered, caring more about how we sound than who we are serving. The spirituality of poetic practice in preaching needs to hold on to a vision of the performative as something that is offered to God and seeks the good of the congregation, not the glory of the preacher. We may, after all, preach in the tongues of angels and have not love. The Gaelic poet Fearghas MacFhionnlaigh warns of this when he writes of 'the mask of the universe having slipped, so there is no longer any correlation between beauty and truth'.[1] Here we rejoin the anxieties some express about performance – that it could be something false, a mask we hide behind, a front. There is no way to insure against this,

---

1 From his long Gaelic poem printed in English translation as 'The Midge' in *Cencrastus* no. 10, Autumn 1982, pp. 28–33

although we might note that boring, prosaic preachers may be as vulnerable to a lack of integrity as artsy, showy ones.

When poetics and performativity are important to us, we need to think about acquiring skills to enrich our practice. Drama classes, movement classes, voice classes and creative writing classes all become potential routes to deepening and developing our own practice. Techniques and exercises from those disciplines are already integrated into many homiletics courses. We learn how to use language from others – from novelists, playwrights, poets, liturgists, the translators of the King James Bible, journalists, rappers, songwriters.

As with our voices, not all of us will be as effective at this as some of us are. Part of finding our voice is knowing when being a bad poet will get in the way of our being a good preacher. We are not all going to be Gil Scott-Heron or Walt Whitman, Sylvia Plath or Maya Angelou. The poetics of our preaching is using language as well as we can, to sound like ourselves and perform the gospel truth we are called to bear witness to. A plainer style will work better than a purple style and give a better witness to beauty if it speaks simply rather than evoking cringes.

# 3.7 How long (has this been going on)

Or, as my mother would say, how long is a piece of string! Talking of my ninety-one-year old mother, for her and her friends Jean and Margaret the length of sermons at their local Baptist church is a constant source of comment. Jean's indomitable approach, while shaking the preacher's hand as she left church, was to look him in the eye and say 'You were a wee bit long again this morning!'

The length of sermons is a mysterious thing. Some seventeenth- and eighteenth-century Church of Scotland parish churches contained a bracket on the pulpit for an hourglass to be placed in, so that the sand would run through as the preacher did his work. The lore is that hearts would sink if the preacher reached out and turned it over, when the sand had already trickled through once. Turning the hourglass over required a lot of confidence in the importance of what you had already said and had yet to say (or, perhaps more commonly, a lack of self-awareness).

Fast forwarding to the twenty-first century, stereotypes still attach to different denominations and traditions. High Church Episcopalians are known for 6–9 minutes, while Low Church Anglicans can deliver 15–30 minutes. Some conservative Presbyterians think nothing of 40 minutes, while most of the rest of us seem to average out at 15–20 minutes. Methodists are a foreign country to me, though one I'm open to visiting in the future. Some preachers are adamant that if something can't be said in 8 minutes you shouldn't be trying to say it at all. Here again, issues of both quality and performativity come into play. I have sat through 8-minute sermons that seemed to last an eternity, and been spellbound for 40 minutes, unconscious of time, wishing a sermon to last longer. Questions of sermon length can take on a different character when they are set in the context of effective performance, so that it can become as odd and reductive to ask a naked question about the length of a sermon as it might be to ask it of a poem or a play. It depends on what you are trying to do and how you are trying to do it. Sam Wells talks about sometimes singing during a sermon, usually a fragment or a verse of a song, while emphasising that he does not count himself a gifted singer. He does it, if I remember his explanation rightly, because of the performative element it adds, the way it disrupts and supplements speech, shifts the voice of the sermon, and changes the flow of emotion. African-American friends have talked to me about how within the (co-producing) rhythms of call and response, a congregation may urge a preacher to keep going longer or to bring it home sooner! Co-production definitely counts here, as congregations can develop expectations of sermon length, which mean they resist having their patience tested or their desires short-changed. The capacities of children in the service or of their Sunday school teachers outside the service may also be a practical factor. The key consideration is not to be lazy or self-indulgent. The Eutychus factor (Acts 20:7–12) is always worth bearing in mind ...

# 3.8 Feel it with me

There are surprisingly few books written about crafting language for use in worship, but one fine one, *Worship Words*, was produced by Debra and Ron Rienstra in 2009. The whole book is a great resource for liturgists and preachers and ideal for use in worship and preaching classes. I want, with permission, to borrow one phrase from their chapter on 'Authenticity', and a short panel section by Ron on preaching called 'Feel It With Me Now'. Written out of his experience of teaching classes on preaching, he reflects on how students, and I would say preachers more generally, can be averse to thinking about 'the emotional contours of their sermons, about deliberately shaping their language in order to solicit an emotional response from their congregations'.[1] Fully aware of concerns about 'manipulation' Ron gently points out how a sermon is also an emotional journey, one that can be led with integrity. We have discussed the 'what is the sermon about?' and 'what is the sermon doing?' questions. He adds this question, 'what do I want people to feel at this point in the sermon?'

The phrase 'feel it with me' has become one of the key phrases that surface in my mind when I am preparing a sermon, or working with students to review their sermons. This is another part of the performative dimension of preaching, which is mediated by the poetics of the sermon and the dynamics of its delivery. In older traditions of rhetoric, this is the role of *pathos*, alongside logos and ethos. Yes, it has to be authentic;

---

1 Rienstra and Rienstra (2009), p. 96.

no, it shouldn't be manipulative or exploitative. Preachers are meant to mediate and embody emotion, in ways that evoke emotion in those who listen. In my own reformed tradition, the (problematic) *Westminster Directory for the Publick Worship of God* from 1645 enjoins those leading congregational prayer to do it in such a way as 'stirs up suitable affections', and this surely applies just as much to preaching as to praying.

I suspect our response to this question has a lot to do with the preaching cultures we are most familiar with and most commonly exposed to. In North America, the long-established traditions of TV evangelism – of brash, showy and even hysterical forms of Pentecostal or independent preaching – may mean that listeners in mainstream churches feel they see too much 'over-emotional' and over-hyped preaching. The links between evoking emotion and soliciting money also display various forms of corruption and cruelty. However, in Scotland and the UK more generally, I tend to feel the opposite is true. When I hear preaching in Presbyterian or Episcopalian churches, I often feel there is a lack of passion and emotional intensity. Preaching styles too often convey detachment, lack of confidence or conviction – almost the opposite of 'feel it with me'.

As a student I listened to Scottish evangelical and reformed preachers like William Still, Eric Alexander and Donald Macleod, whose preaching was charged with emotion and conviction. Perhaps the best years of my life in the pew were in Hackney, East London, under the ministry of Revd Dr Lance Stone, later of Westminster College, Cambridge, and now at the English Reformed Church in Amsterdam. Lance's preaching was marked by integrity, but also by intensity. When I think of 'feel it with me', it is his sermons I think of first. The Welsh poet and clergyman R. S. Thomas, in his poem 'The Chapel', describes a disused chapel settling down into the grass:

here once on an evening like this,
in the darkness that was about
his hearers, a preacher caught fire
and burned steadily before them
with a strange light, so that they saw
the splendour of the barren mountains
about them and sang their amens
fiercely, narrow but saved
in a way that men are not now.

Lance's preaching was never narrow, but I swear there were
Sundays in the little red brick reformed church in Hackney,
East London, when he caught fire and burned before us.
Thomas's image of the burning bush evokes the sense of divine
presence coming through the preached word of God. I am sure,
without those years of listening to Lance, I would never have
become a preacher.

Lest it seem like this might only come in one form, I would cite
as another example my colleague Professor Heather Walton,
formed as a lay preacher in the Methodist Church in the North
of England. Heather has a soft pulpit voice, but her preaching
is charged with emotional intensity, because she uses language
so deftly, precisely and forcefully. She can powerfully evoke
scenes and experiences through extraordinary lush and sensual
description, can render raw emotion, is fierce in her articu-
lation of anger, outrage and resistance. There is a relentless
tenderness about her preaching. We feel it with her.

# 3.9 Head, heart (gut), hand

The Waldorf-Steiner movement in education is well known for using the phrase 'head, heart, hand' to describe its holistic and integrated approach to learning. Anglican theologian Sam Wells has helpfully applied this to preaching. With a slight twist, Wells suggests that a sermon should offer something for the head, heart, *gut* and hand; this draws on the conceptuality of the Hebrew Bible to add a term that brings a sense of grittiness, urgency and painful reality.[1]

This aspiration is not new in the history of preaching or of classical rhetoric, where *logos* and *pathos* were both essential components. It is an aspiration to forms of preaching that are intellectually challenging, emotionally rich and conscious of the need for faith to be accompanied by works. That can all sound rather conventional in the end and there is something fitting about that, rebuking the presumption that we have discovered much that is new about preaching since the days of the apostles. When Wells inserts his 'gut' term into the Steiner trio, what gives it force is the way he uses it to rethink what is assumed and what is omitted from the conventional aspirations to a 'holistic homiletic'. He points, for example, to issues around physical and mental health being deep and common preoccupations that our pulpits are too often reticent or silent about.[2] This rethinking of what might be repressed in

---

1 Wells (2001), Introduction.

2 I am drawing here on my recollection of a lecture he gave in Cambridge in 2011.

our pulpits seems, on reflection, to be a contextual task that has to be done again in every generation. We are familiar with the truism that the Victorians were in denial about sex and were obsessed with death, while today we have reversed that.

The value of this three- or four-fold formula comes not because it is new, since it is in fact very old. It comes from our using it to think through once again, in our time, what is unsaid, unthought, unacknowledged. In my preaching classes, we tackle this under the heading of 'the things we never say' and link this to 'the texts we never choose'. Picking up one of the earliest reflections in this book, lectionary preaching that explores widely across the canon can play a part in directing attention to issues and ideas that might otherwise be missed. However, that will only take us so far, because what also matters is the hermeneutic we bring to those texts. Some of the blind spots in our heremeneutic, which become blind spots or quiet zones in our preaching, are given a corrective from critical liberationist perspectives, but other instances of collective repression or denial may not show up so clearly in those lights. Every radical tradition also has its own blind spots, its own sins of omission, its own unthought, unfelt and unpreached. Head, heart (gut) and hand can be a useful set of lenses, but we also need a way of circling back to question what counts as head, heart (gut) and hand for us, and what doesn't, and why.

# 3.10 Getting out of the way

In Part 4, 'Living', I will go on to mention some things that are in tension with what I am about say here, but hopefully the tension will be productive. Here I want to rehearse the caution about being preachers 'who like the sound of their own voices'. Different ministries within the Church bring different besetting sins and bespoke temptations with them. As I write this, I am thinking about C. S. Lewis and *The Screwtape Letters*, which remains one of the wittiest and sharpest exposés of how we incubate and incarnate particular faults and failings within the particular circumstances of our own lives and characters. It might be interesting to compile a more comprehensive 'sin list' for preachers, and I will add a few of these 'sins' in Part 4, but for now I want to focus on self-importance, remembering what Paul writes in Romans 12:3, 'by the grace given to me I say to everyone among you not to think of yourself more highly than you ought to think, but to think with sober judgment, each according to the measure of faith that God has assigned'.

Preachers, particularly in our use of illustrations, stories and cultural references, are called to walk a fine line between offering ourselves as personal mediators of the word and getting in the way. In one sense, our selves are all we have to work with but, resorting to the proverbial again, we can be 'too full of ourselves'. The symptoms of this, which Screwtape might delight to point out to Wormwood, include a tendency to find ourselves more interesting than we are and to overshare about our own lives and experience. I have listened to preachers in response to whom I felt the Holy Spirit urging me to shout out 'It's not all about you.' The very same preachers might well have been most likely to refer in the next breath to *soli Deo Gloria*, but in my experience that rhetoric is no insurance against this particular disease. The epidemiology here shows it to be more prevalent among those who already feel powerful – that is, straight white men. In his poem 'The Mad Farmer Liberation Front', Wendell Berry writes: 'So long as women do not go cheap for power, please women more than men.'[1] We need to remember that men have inherited centuries of bad pulpit habits, which came bundled with a sense of entitlement to preach.

As preachers we need to keep a check on our egos, allowing them to keep on checking in with our empathy, our solidarity and our discretion. Whatever the answer is to the question of what this sermon is doing, it should never be simply boosting, stroking or parading our egos. Nor should it be washing our dirty linen in public, pleading for congregational sympathy, or trying too hard to please people or make them like us.

When we speak from the privileged space of the pulpit (or its functional equivalent), we need to find unobtrusive ways to be fully present. As the old (preacher facing) sign in many a small-time pulpit used to say, 'Sir, we would see Jesus.'

---

1 www.counterpointpress.com/dd-product/the-mad-farmer-poems.

# PART 4

# Living

# 4.1  Pathos – being human

In this final part of the book, I try to reflect on how the work of preaching gets folded in to our daily living, returning to some of the themes about being ourselves and being appropriately self-conscious about that.

Preaching is work for ordinary women and men, called by God and the Church. It is not work for angels and we are not angels. If, as Karl Barth says over and over again, the word of God establishes us in our true humanity, makes us more truly and fully ourselves, we might even dare to hope that, as preachers, this word would not be far from us, but 'near us, in our mouths and in our hearts, so that we can do it' (Rom. 10:8; Deut. 30:11–14).

The preaching we are called to continues the preaching of Jesus Christ. The prologue to John's Gospel names him using a term that was key to ancient rhetoric – he is the *logos*. The Gospels also show Jesus continually demonstrating what Jurgen Moltmann, following Abraham Heschel, calls 'the *pathos* of God'.[1] Jesus became flesh and lived among us. Jesus came to feel it with us. He is able to sympathise with our weaknesses (Heb. 4:15). It is as the one who lives with us, who sympathises with us, that Jesus preaches to us.

The architecture of the pulpit is loaded with danger for us if it goes beyond a functional raising of us up to be seen and heard

---

1 Moltmann (1974).

and removes us from those we speak to. This threatens the fundamental need for Christ-likeness in our preaching, that we speak as those who live with, feel with and feel for the people to whom we preach. The minimum standard held up for our preaching is that it should be 'speaking the truth in love' (Eph. 4:15).

As preachers we should learn from the criticisms directed against those politicians who struggle to 'talk human'. Learning to preach is learning to 'talk human'. We are at our most human when we are full of grace and truth, when we speak in love. Compassion, sympathy, solidarity, empathy and mercy are utterly basic to the work of homiletics, which makes this yet another site within a reflection on preaching that must drive us to prayer. When God is in our mouths and in our speaking, we sound human.

# 4.2 Look at me when I'm talking to you

Embracing our humanity as preachers means learning to make peace with some very basic, inescapable truths about ourselves, which we often struggle to be at home with. It means, as we said when reflecting on hubris and self-importance, being present with and to the people we preach to.

In the spring of 2010, the Yugoslavian-born performance artist Marina Abramović performed *The Artist Is Present* at the Museum of Modern Art in New York City. Abramović sat immobile in the atrium of the museum for many hours each day, while people were invited to come one at a time and sit opposite her, making eye contact with her, but not speaking or touching. Videos of the performance are available online and are compelling viewing, with your eye being drawn in turn to the artist, to the seated companion, to those standing waiting in line for their turn, to those standing around watching. Some of those who sit opposite stay longer than others, some smile, most are quietly serious and attentive, some sit and weep.

The first work of the preacher is to show up, to be present, as our Lord showed up and was present. To show up is to be there, in the body you are, dressed as you are, looking like you do. To show up is to face people and to invite their gaze and their attention. It is a seldom discussed and reflected upon aspect of preaching that you stand, or sit if in a wheelchair, *in front of* the congregation. There is something exposing about preaching. Even if you are clothed in clerical dress, robed in the office of preacher, you are still there before the church. People look at you when you preach, watch you as they listen to you. As the historic bans on women preaching and presiding at sacraments were being lifted across mainstream Protestant denominations in the twentieth century, it was clear that for some men,[1] the imperative of gazing at a woman was a problem to them. In the course of church debates about ordaining women, some men said crass and revealing things about finding women in the pulpit or at the table sexually distracting.[2] It was clear that accepting *the woman is present* was challenging for them as was accepting that the woman was present *in a place of discursive power*, with the right and call to speak.

To be present in our humanity is always to be present in our specific humanity, as male or female, as old or young, black or white, short or tall. It is not always easy to be seen and heard, although it can become easier over time. The adult rebuke that many of us will remember from a teacher or parent, 'Look at me when I am talking to you!', becomes our own implicit invitation to those we stand or sit in front of. Abramović's work, in its deadly simplicity, stripping away words and movement, reveals that to us. The preacher is present.

To reflect on this may seem to invite trouble. We will become self-conscious, we say. That concern summons insecurity, embarrassment, unease. What good will it do to think about this? My point in raising it here is that we may be wise to

---

1 It was a complicated and conflicted thing for some women too ...

2 For some men, the 'pulpit' is very obviously a place of sexual power as well as rhetorical power. It is a place where they strut and smoulder; some exploit this outside the pulpit, but many are boosted by it. Yet, with a typical combination of presumption and lack of insight, few of those who suggested women might be sexually distracting would imagine men could be. This also has to do with how men don't own or acknowledge their bodies, although they exploit them endlessly.

consider from the beginning some of the dynamics of drawing attention, of being seen, of being heard. We will be forced to realise that there is always a politics of positioning within the choreography of worship; that assuming a prominent place, from which we can be seen and heard, may call us to certain virtues: humility, courage, pride, confidence, vulnerability. We may have to claim or acknowledge the power that comes with this work.

The acknowledgement of our own bodies also makes us confront questions about what it means for preaching to be 'spiritual' work. Many in our congregations grew up with highly dualistic orientations, singing 'make my flesh life melt away' and being catechised into a mindset in which bodies were a problem that spiritual experience freed us from. With particular help from womanist and feminist theology and from theologies of disability, we are slowly learning how to think out of and live into a theology of embodiment. My pitch here is that homiletics has its own work to do and its own contribution to make within this area of theology. It is not only Biblical literature and sermons that have form, preachers do too. There is one mediator, but we are all media. When most of us are formally called to a preaching ministry by the Church, the 'ordination' or 'commissioning' is done 'by the laying on of hands'. It is an embodied ritual, other bodies touching 'this body', claiming and recognising it for the ministry of the word. If we can grow in our understanding of the 'somatics' of preaching, if we as preachers can live in, with and as our bodies, it will have profound consequences for how we speak about the lived, embodied experience of others. It will have consequences for how we think about what it means to be spiritual and to seek spiritual transformation. It will also change how we understand the politics of worship, because bodies carry political charge and salience, which is why female bodies and black bodies can act as triggers for those within the Church whose power they threaten.

In 2 Corinthians 4:7, Paul writes of the treasure of the gospel being carried in 'earthen vessels', the bodies of the believers/apostles, and develops this by talking about mental and physical suffering, but also about the life of Jesus being made visible in our bodies. We are into the somatic homiletics of Sam Wells's preaching for the 'gut' – the bodies we preach in are bodies that get sick, get old, get depressed, get too fat or too thin, get drunk, embrace one another, delight in great-tasting food, have orgasms, die.

Preaching comes from and goes to embodied living. To be present can be a costly thing, in particular to be present in such a visible, up front, looked at and scrutinised way. I know from talking to other preachers that I am not the only one who regularly feels emotionally drained by preaching, over-exposed, ready to walk away and curl up in a darkened room. We risk ourselves in preaching. Sometimes (often ...) we disappoint ourselves.

Finally, there is the opposite of presence. There are ways of not showing up, of phoning it in, of going there without being there. If those go beyond the odd few lost Sundays and start to accumulate, we need to go and talk to somebody we trust, because that is a sign that our ministry is in danger.

In all of this, we have to do with an emerging theme and field for homiletics, but one which is full of challenge and promise. In 2 Corinthians 4:6, Paul speaks of the light of the gospel which shines in the face of Jesus Christ. When we preach, we preach in the name of the God, who in Jesus has said, 'Look at me when I am talking to you.'

# 4.3 Ethos – trust me, I'm a preacher

The third term in Aristotle's trio, alongside logos and pathos, is *ethos*. Ethos, linked to ethics, takes us into the realm of virtue and of the character of the speaker. Aristotle observed that we more readily believe speakers when we perceive them to be good people or people of good character.[1] I pick up again here on some of the themes in sections 3.2 and 3.10 above – on being yourself and not being above yourself. Our character, ethics and integrity as preachers are hugely important. These things matter to God, to those we preach to, to the world looking on and listening in, to the Church and to ourselves.

The first word here is honesty: if you fake it, you break it. From the beginning we need to decide for honesty, pray for honesty and put ourselves within structures of accountability that will help us to remain honest. We are more likely to commit to that if we understand how toxic it is to our own souls, to lie and dissemble and pretend. It is a sure way of hollowing ourselves out. If we seek that route to gaining our lives, we will lose them. The author of Colossians puts it plainly in 3:9, 'Do not lie to one another.'

The outright lie will be at the extreme end of the spectrum; the more common temptation is to pretend to be better or wiser

---

1 'Persuasion is achieved by the speaker's personal character when the speech is so spoken as to make us think him credible. We believe good men more fully and more readily than others: this is true generally whatever the question is, and absolutely true where exact certainty is impossible and opinions are divided ... his character may almost be called the most effective means of persuasion he possesses' (Aristotle, *Rhetoric*, 1.2.1356a.4–12).

or more pious than we really are and to do some of that pretending and dissembling in the pulpit for the sake of effect. We are tempted to do that because we realise Aristotle was right – ethos matters. I think of this as our attempt as preachers to live beyond our means, and I believe firmly that if we do this habitually it will break our ministries. We need the moral and spiritual discipline as preachers to be honest with ourselves and with our congregations.

If we live in a family, the first place we will see the cost of dishonesty is likely to be on the faces and in the eyes of our husband, or wife or children. They will grow to pity, resent or even despise us if we are saints in the pulpit and selfish egotists at home.

No matter how seductive it may seem, to pretend that we are closer to God, more prayerful, more filled with the Holy Spirit, purer in heart and eye and speech, etc. than we know ourselves to be is death in our veins. We have to be honest in the pulpit, recognising, as I said earlier, that this does not mean over-disclosing or washing dirty linen in public.

Now of course there is the whole of the gospel to be set against this and all the riches of the grace and mercy of our Lord Jesus Christ. As Philip Yancey says, 'grace means there is nothing I can do to make God love me more, and nothing I can do to make God love me less'.[2] Every time we open our mouths to preach, we are relying on the justifying, forgiving, redeeming love of God in Christ; we are preaching as unworthy servants, clothed in an alien righteousness, which is ours by grace through faith. We are earthen vessels, but we have 'treasure'! There is nothing that can separate us from the love of God, but there are things we can do, or not do, that can and should separate us from the work of preaching. There are moral and

---

2 Yancey (1997).

ethical failures, screw ups and follies, which in no way put us beyond the grace and love of God, who always comes to find us in the far country, even the farthest country; but these may mean we have to get out of the pulpit, for our own good and for that of other people. These failures may mean that we need some time to close the gap, to rebuild a shattered ethos, to get to a place where we can stand ourselves again, where we and others can bear to hear the sound of our own preaching voice. For some of us, there may never be a return to the pulpit and that may be a source of great sadness, because a gift has been wasted, but it may still be the best outcome. For those who do return, the best judge of when to do it will be when the word of absolution spoken over them by our colleagues, or by a bishop or moderator, is joined by a word that re-calls, that says you are ready to come back now, to be restored, we want you to preach among us again. Without that and without it being echoed by those who know us best, attempts at premature self-rehabilitation do not come from wisdom.

I believe that honesty in the pulpit is protective of our ethos and integrity. Sometimes we should say, 'I struggle with this passage' or 'I don't know the answer' – we should acknowledge how hard it is to live with some tensions, to struggle against some temptations. There may be topics on which we will be unable to preach because of our own struggles or vulnerabilities, but there may be someone else who can come and preach, whose ethos will free them to speak in ways that bless us and our congregation.

So far, I have spoken very personally about ethos, but there is a social and political dimension to this as well. Early in the book I quoted Bonhoeffer's comment about speaking up for the Jews; that is a comment about ethos. We know that we have to walk the walk if we are going to talk the talk. To speak from the side I know best, this matters profoundly in relationships between white preachers and people of colour who are colleagues, parishioners or congregation members. When I think of those who have been role models for me, I think of Revd Nibs Stroupe of Oakhurst Presbyterian Church in Decatur, Atlanta, Georgia, who was pastor to various friends of mine. I met him, heard him preach, and read his remarkable book, written with Inez Fleming, *While We Run This Race*.[3] In London, from my time in the United Reformed Church, Revd John Campbell and Revd Francis Ackroyd won deep respect from black colleagues and parishioners for the ethos of their ministries of solidarity and their anti-racist work. When we lived in one of the poorest areas of Glasgow, where the divides within a mostly white community were to do with class, poverty and sectarianism, Church of Scotland deacon Janet Anderson showed me over and over again the profound trust, and the quiet spiritual authority, that were made possible by her ethos of living and standing alongside the poor.

Ethos, then, is political as well as personal. Our political ethos will be read from our sermons and will be betrayed by what we say or don't say and by how we express ourselves. If we never show signs of awareness of where communities experience injustice, of where people need recognition and respect, of how power works, of how money works, of who gets trampled on, of who perpetrates violence and who is the victim of it, and if our preaching doesn't show any evidence that we *see* the world other people live in every day, that has consequences for our ethos as preachers.

Finally, since this is about truth and justice, we need to remember that ethos is about our relationship with God, is about what the Lord thinks of us and requires of us: 'to do justice, to love mercy and to walk humbly with our God'.

---

3 Stroupe and Fleming (1995).

# 4.4 It's a gig

I touched earlier on the unease some people feel about the performative aspects of preaching, because they associate that rubric for thinking and talking about preaching with a lack of authenticity or spirituality. I want to return to this as another aspect of the humanity of preaching. Many of us, probably most, get scared, apprehensive, nervous before we preach, in exactly the same way as people get nervous before any performance – in sport, music or public speaking. Just as in those settings, there is a spectrum of how that affects our performance, from being crippled by nerves to being fuelled by adrenaline, with the full range of options in between.

My experience, and I think that of most preachers, is that practice and time does help. I am less nervous now than I was in my earliest years of preaching and that is a good thing. If we suffer badly from nerves or stage-fright,[1] we should find ways to work on that and not be embarrassed to seek help, coaching or therapy. If we have a call, we can hope that God and the Church will help us to fulfil that, but if it proves too difficult we may have to stop preaching (or preaching regularly) for our own good and that of the Church. Sometimes people offer pious clichés that insist God will always fix things – it is important for us and for our preaching that we understand God does not always fix things. Issues with our mental health or personal confidence can end a preaching ministry, just as

---

1 Canadian Mennonite homiletician Allan Rudy-Froese is doing research on stage-fright among preachers.

issues with our physical health can. It is not a failure to be ill, nor does it mean we never had a call in the first place. It just means we got ill.

The positive side of thinking about performance is that once we make our peace with that language and conceptuality, it may act as an invitation into some more creative, exploratory and even playful ways of preaching. Once again, some of us will be better at this than others. Some folk are natural mimics; some use humour better than others; some are better storytellers; some are better poets; some can use the range of their voices better than others; some use gesture and body language more effectively; some make more effective use of call and response, including their interaction with musicians while preaching. All of these are aspects of performance, are skills, gifts and abilities that can be brought to the ministry of the word. As T. S. Eliot says in 'Choruses from *"The Rock"*':

> LORD, shall we not bring these gifts to Your service?
> Shall we not bring to Your service all our powers
> For life, for dignity, grace and order,
> And intellectual pleasures of the senses?
> The LORD who created must wish us to create
> ... You must not deny the body.[2]

Preaching does not depend on the fullness of these gifts, but if we have them, we can bring them. To call preaching a 'gig', does not mean we are inauthentic or unspiritual when we 'perform' (although we may be). It does mean, though, we have to reflect on our practice. Does it feel authentic to us? Are we exploring areas of performance that serve and enhance the word? Are we just showing off and doing things because we can and because we get easy reactions or responses? Are we embarrassingly bad at the aspect of performance we persist with? If so, we should

---

2 T. S. Eliot, 'Choruses from *"The Rock"* IX', in *Collected Poems 1909–1962*, Faber & Faber, 1963.

stop attempting it unless our capacity shifts dramatically. As my teenage kids are fond of saying: 'Dad, never do/say that ...'

Finally, it is worth noting that some of the bias against performance and the inability to examine it well reflects the cultural and racial biases of white preachers, academics and congregations. Tellingly, of course, what this assumes is that something that may be other to them *is* performance, *is* performative, while the way they do things is not. The truth? It's all performative. The incarnation and preaching of Jesus Christ was performative. That reminds us of another profound truth about performance, which is where we go next.

# 4.5 God is with you in the pulpit

I have a vivid memory of talking to a friend when I was a student about a preacher whose sermon had made a huge impact on me. He knew the preacher well so I asked him – probably the wrong question – something like how does he preach like that? I hardly remember the question, but the answer has always stayed with me: 'He has an unshakeable belief that God is with him in the pulpit.' Again, I might want to nuance it now, given that I have a more chastened sense of how many things are 'shakeable' in our lives, but there was something about that emphasis on believing that God is with us in preaching that has been enduring and encouraging for me.

Yes, preaching is a gig and yes, we need to reckon with the fullness and frailty of our humanity in preaching, but we do not believe that we are the only ones involved in the performance or that it depends entirely upon us. One image I return to here is the image of Jesus at his baptism in the Jordan. The Spirit descends like a dove, the voice comes from heaven – the whole scene is a picture, a performance in fact, of divine benediction and accompaniment, of God being with Jesus at the outset of his ministry. We are not alone in preaching. We are present, but the Holy Trinity is present too.

I am only an occasional poet. I fool myself that if I preached less I might write more poetry – and I hope for a time in my life when that will be true! That thought, of God being with us when we preach, lies behind this poem:

## The Minister Preaches His Sermon

'As clowns yearn to play Hamlet,
so I have wanted to write a treatise on God.
This book, however, is not it.'
J. I. Packer – *Knowing God* (from the Prologue)


no one knows better than you
both why and that I am a fool,
or what the many reasons are
why this is true.


not least
it is because again today
I've spoken of the mysteries of God
as one who knows.


I never warmed to Packer's book,
but liked his prologue, and his love of jazz.


As Barth said, talk of God is what we must and cannot do.
Us preachers, we are always just the clowns
who play at Hamlet for a day.
Unless, we can believe that there is more in play.


His son spoke movingly of Eric's preparation,
How the Word weighed heavy on him, weighed him down.
And I believe it; since beside such men
I feel a light weight, fly weight,
amateur orator, preaching dilettante.
(Although it was not his technique or skill.
But somehow it was clear, the Word would have its way
   with him,
would have mysterious free course through his own words.)

So Packer's prologue is the epilogue for all our books.
This is not it, these words are not the word.
But back to Barth:
By some accommodating miracle, sometimes
The heft of truth outweighs our flimsiness.

There is no point to pulpit thundering
No safety in poetic skill or fiery rhetoric.
No authenticity in your 'experience'.
Absent the weighting, Godot-esque,
It is all just fooling around. But wait.

If '*praedicatio verbi dei est verbum dei*' then,
Fools may be preachers when the fire comes down.
And we may even dare to preach again,
If Christ will say, Send in the clowns.

# 4.6 God-talk – other ways to hear the word

God-talk is more than preaching. This is a book on preaching, so up until now everything I have written has had a fairly conventional view of preaching and the sermon in mind. But there is more to talking about God and to hearing the word of God in church than can or should be done in preaching. Over the last three decades, I have been heavily involved in congregations associated with *alternative worship*[1] and the *emerging church*.[2]

Something I noted in previous books reflecting on that involvement is that many of those I collaborated with and learned from were fairly hostile towards preaching. Their suspicions were usually based on their experiences of preachers they had found boring, or patronising or authoritarian; sometimes all three together. In the collective forms of worship preparation that took place in these new church spaces, it was very rare for anyone to then be allowed to speak for longer than 5 minutes in a service. People would work in groups responding to Biblical passages or themes through music, visual images, ritual and environment. The final service would be the product of a shared, communal hermeneutic encounter with the text. No one individual was given the task of sharing the word.

---

1 Baker and Gay (2003).
2 Gay (2011).

Alongside those, I have been regularly involved with friends in the Iona Community and Wild Goose Resource Group events. John Bell, who is a leading figure in these, was one of my supervisors during ministry training and has been a mentor and friend ever since. Although he is a very fine preacher and his ministry is affirmed by his colleagues in those groups, there is a pervasive concern in events they run to encourage reflection on Scripture and theology from the whole body of believers. Often one of those leading, after the scripture has been read, will invite people to turn to their neighbour and respond to one or more simple open questions about the passage.

In both of these examples, there is a direct challenge to the politics of conventional worship and ministry, which includes a challenge to the role and the power of the preacher. I think I have said enough to make it clear that I affirm the ministry of preachers, but I also want to affirm this challenge to it. Preachers have had, and continue to have, too much power in our churches and it has been corrupting for them and debilitating for those not called to this ministry,[3] who have too often had agency and opportunity kept from them. I believe in preaching, but I believe in it within a broad ecology of church life, in which there are many different forms of God-talk and of encounter with the Scriptures.

When I told people I was writing a book on preaching, some were fairly sceptical. They were not keen on preaching and dismayed that anyone should waste time writing a book about it. I hope that for some of them, the idea of preaching as poetics and performance may be one way in which they can move beyond a resentment of the power dynamics and the opportunity for the wider Church. If it happens, a rehabilitation of preaching for them will, I believe, have to involve seeing preaching find and take its place within a range of church life and practices. Those of us who preach may need to think more about how to

---

3 Those who are called 'lay people' in some traditions.

explain, justify and commend preaching to those who doubt its value. We will also need to listen to critical voices and reflect on them. Preaching comes with a lot of baggage from the Church's past and people have suffered a lot at the mouths of preachers. We who preach need to remember that.

# 4.7 Be preached to

Preachers need to listen to preaching, they need to be aware of how other people preach, they need to remember what it feels like to listen to a sermon, and they need to keep learning through that listening. If you are part of a clergy or preaching team in your congregation, that may happen easily and naturally, but within my denomination and other mainstream denominations increasing numbers of ministers and preachers are looking after multiple congregations and may be preaching for more than forty Sundays a year. That might only seem to leave holidays to hear other preachers, but the wonders of the internet mean that it is possible to tune in and listen to preachers from all over the world on any given day of the week and at any time. The Center for Excellence in Preaching at Calvin Theological Seminary has an audio sermon archive and many congregations worldwide keep recordings of their services on a website accessible to all comers.

Although we may miss the rounded experience of hearing a sermon within the context of an act of worship at which we are present, listening in may also be an effective way of checking and reflecting on how we are 'fed' by preaching, on what nourishes and inspires us. If we have been helped by our own theological education and ministry experience to become critical and reflective hearers of sermons, we may find that we sometimes struggle with our own highly judgmental instincts about preaching. That may be inevitable and even healthy up to a point, but we may also need to rediscover instincts for generosity and sympathy. If we are working within a team or if we are mentoring and supervising those learning to preach, we need to remember that there were people who, in a phrase I heard from my friend Calum Macleod, describing the congregation at Fourth Pres in Chicago, 'listened us into ministry'.[1] Few of us emerged as the fully formed article and many of us tried the patience of folk in the pews while we were learning to preach. The skill of offering constructive criticism and helpful feedback is always needed within the life of the Church.

Listening to others may have another unintended effect, that of making us depressed about our own preaching. Again, that may sometimes be inevitable and may be one of the ways the Spirit trains us in the virtue of humility. Hopefully, if we start to feel bad about how we preach, we will be open to finding ways to keep on learning, developing and growing. There are often conferences, summer schools and continuing ministerial development opportunities available that we could take advantage of. We might choose to spend a sabbatical or a period of study leave refreshing our approach to preaching.

A final thought is that if we are one of the regular up-front leaders and preachers in our congregation, it is good for other people to see us 'in the pews', listening, weighing what is said, and opening our lives to the word. It may also be that this can be part of enabling our own congregation to hear a broader range of voices from the pulpit. If they mostly hear us preaching, it might be good for us and them to hear a man preach, if we are a woman, or a woman preach, if we are a man. It might be good for all of us to sit and listen to a colleague from another denomination or tradition preach in our congregation. If we are young, then it might be good to hear an older preacher; if we are old, then it might be good for them and us to hear a younger preacher.

---

1 An echo of Nelle Morton's 'hearing each other to speech' quoted by Beverley Wildung Harrison in Loades (1990), p. 204.

For all these reasons and more, we as preachers need to be preached to.

# 4.8 Preaching in love

I have a clear and heartwarming memory of hearing the late John Stott quote a preacher of bygone years who said, 'by the grace of God I have been able to fall in love with my congregation'. Falling in love with the congregation as a whole is a safer option than falling for individual members, unless of course you are free to do so. To pick up on earlier comments about speaking the truth in love, preaching belongs within a relationship of loving regard for those we are preaching to. Love opens us out to the other, it seeks their good, it takes care to see them fed, watered, affirmed, restored. It draws us out from our own preoccupations with ourselves, with our success or failure, with our prerogatives and position, and it reinforces the idea that preaching is *ministry*, is service.

This is another dimension of being present to people, of allowing ourselves and how we preach to be shaped by their needs, their griefs, their struggles and troubles. Preaching requires a soft heart, although this sometimes needs to be held within a thick skin. I remember as a student reading words that Jim Wallis wrote of and to the Church; words that have stayed with me and come back to me often: 'We have nothing more to share with the world than what we are sharing with each other.'[1] Our preaching must be the work of love, and if we – or others – find our preaching to be loveless, or lacking in love, that is cause for reflection on our own experience of the love of

---

1 Wallis (1981), p. 130.

God *and* of how we are held in loving relationships within the life of the Church.

Planning a year's preaching is also planning a year of 'loving people in the word'. This is not (only) soft or sentimental; love speaks the truth and love can be tough. I often think of womanist theologian Beverley Wildung Harrison's classic essay 'The Power of Anger in the Work of Love'.[2] The pulpit can and should be a place from which angry words are said, remembering the counsel of Ephesians 4:26 to 'be angry but sin not'.[3] There is much to be angry about in the world that the preacher is called to see and speak into, but there is also a great need for that anger to be enlisted and made non-violent by the work of love.

Perhaps more than any other single question about our work, the question as to whether we have preached with love and in love is the one most likely to silence us and send us to our knees. That is as it should be. There is mission, David Bosch says, because God loves people.[4] Preaching only makes sense and finds its place within the *missio dei*, and since it is love that drives that mission, it is love that should fire our preaching.

2 Reprinted in Loades (1990), pp. 194ff.
3 Here I quote the classic rendering from the KJV.
4 Bosch (1991), p. 392.

# 4.9 Logos – the mind of the preacher

Intellect, understanding, rationality, wisdom, sense, meaning ... The third term in classical rhetoric was *logos*, a word that has its own unique intersection with Christian theology and the theology of preaching. In 1 Corinthians 14:19 Paul makes clear his desire for people to speak in church with 'understanding' – the Greek word is one of a few that has made the crossover into British slang use: to show some 'nous' is to show some practical intelligence.

As someone involved in education for ministry, I sometimes get challenges from church-people about why you have to have a university degree to be ordained as a preacher, given that some of the first apostles were fishermen with little formal education. I find this a persuasive objection to higher education being the exclusive route to ministry. On the other hand, I grew up in the Plymouth Brethren during the years when there was a ban on people going to university, so that most of the preachers were self-taught, self-educated, and cut off from the mainstream of theological tradition and debate. That didn't end well and a lot of the preaching was very poor, some of it *because* of a lack of education and formation.

However, I do want to resist the idea that all preachers should be intellectuals or academics, or people who might like reading a book like this. I think the Church should be willing to call and ordain people who have adequate formation and who can display a Holy Spirit-enriched 'nous' in their preaching. I also think the ecology of ministry within the Church should be diverse, so that we value academic traditions of scholarship, including linguistic, textual and philosophical scholarship. We need a spectrum of people who exercise 'nous' or *phronesis*, 'practical wisdom', ranging from those with little formal education to research professors who are also 'doctors' in Calvin's sense of this word. In between, we need a combination of people encompassing both those who think like engineers or mathematicians and those who think like artists or gardeners. Logos takes flesh in many different ways in our lives and the key concern is that each of these living human words is a disciple of the word made flesh, who is able to 'read',[1] as well as being called and gifted to preach.

Whatever our intellectual capacity, aptitude or style as preachers, we are called to be stewards of that, open to new experiences of learning and formation. I vividly recall as a student Free Church theologian Donald Macleod suggesting in a sermon that there should typically be 'noetic' consequences that flowed from our redemption in Christ. His vision of 'the renewal of our minds'[2] was that across the whole spectrum of the Christian community the work of the Holy Spirit would be to awaken curiosity, to deepen a desire to learn, to open minds to education and draw minds to scholarship. We will all instantly be able to think of depressing counterfactuals, but the words of that (heard not read) sermon have stayed with me over many decades as an inspiration. At its best, the Church has been a powerful advocate of education, founding and supporting educational institutions at every level down through the centuries. A Christian vision of the fullness of life should include a passion for education, a valuing of those who teach and mentor others; a sense that places where people gather

---

1 Or 'hear' God's word to them. Although it would be unusual today, in principle I think it is important to be able to accept that God could use, and has used, illiterate preachers to spread the gospel.

2 Romans 12:2.

to learn – from kindergartens, through primary schools and high schools, to colleges and universities – are hallowed places. It has become counter-cultural in our secularising society to believe that churches can be places of intellectual discovery, of enlightenment and wisdom, where science and scholarship are esteemed, and where the arts are valued and explored. Preaching is one of the key sites within the life of a local church where the culture of that church in relation to *logos* is on display. It is not the only place – Sunday schools and study groups also play a crucial role – but preaching will always set some kind of tone, for good or ill. Integral to all of this should be the Church's concern for justice, peace and the integrity of creation, and the ways this is related to how we 'learn the world'. Brazilian educationalist Paolo Freire, in his famous book *The Pedagogy of the Oppressed*, explored the concept of 'conscientização' (Portuguese) or 'conscientisation':[3] learning to see the world as a place of oppression, where we must struggle to seek justice and transformation. When the *logos* becomes flesh and walks among us, when he goes to the edges of our societies (and their centres), when he sees and hears and smells the world of the poor (and the rich), in all of its goodness and in all of its brokenness, he brings with him a call to relearn the world by the renewing of our minds.

As preachers, it is our discipled learning of the world that is on show on Sundays, and this privilege and burden brings intimidating responsibilities as well as powerful opportunities. Can we show our learning to others without being 'showy', can we share our understanding without sounding superior or being patronising? Can we stretch our own minds and those of others without making some people feel stupid or excluded? The difficult calling of the preacher is often to preach with integrity to a congregation that includes both people with little formal education and people with higher degrees. That will

---

3 Freire (1972), drawing on Frantz Fanon's 1952 use of 'conscienciser' in *Black Skins, White Masks*.

never be easy to fulfil. It will always be shaped by what we think logos, intelligence and wisdom is! It will be helped by our remaining humble and being open to learn ourselves. It will be checked by our being willing to hear and respond to the hearts and minds of those we preach to, which is the (final) topic we turn to.

# 4.10 How was it for you?

Since this is the last section of the book, poetic justice as much as anything else seemed to demand that it was devoted to the voices of those who listen to preaching. There are, though, some important Biblical precedents for completely ignoring the views of the 'preached-to'. It is a common trope in the prophetic writings that the prophet is told to hold to the word they have been given, regardless of opposition. In Ezekiel 3:7–9 the prophet is told:

> But the house of Israel will not listen to you, for they are not willing to listen to me; because all the house of Israel have a hard forehead and a stubborn heart. See, I have made your face hard against their faces, and your forehead hard against their foreheads. Like the hardest stone, harder than flint, I have made your forehead; do not fear them or be dismayed at their looks, for they are a rebellious house … Say to them, 'Thus says the Lord God'; whether they hear or refuse to hear.

It is not impossible that some of us preachers, at certain times in our lives, may receive such a commission from the Lord and, if we do, then I guess we should gird our loins and try to fulfil it. More commonly, we will be serving in a situation where our congregation is God's gift to us and we are called to be attentive to their thoughts and feelings, their judgements and reactions. They are the ones who hear us into speech, who listen us into ministry, who pray for us, who endure our enthusiasms, our limitations and our sense of humour or lack thereof. Given that, the question arises as to what role they play in our preaching?

Some scholars in homiletics have developed detailed scholarly tools for obtaining structured feedback on sermons, and some seminaries require students to get such feedback from their congregations while they are on field placements or student attachments.[1] There is no reason why any preacher who wanted to could not draw on these examples and adapt them for use in their own context. It is increasingly common in the voluntary sector and across industry for managers to undertake 360° assessments, where they seek feedback from those on all sides of their work. It is rarer for preachers, ministers or pastors to do this, but it could be a useful way to refresh our ministry. It might even bring significant encouragement to us as preachers, while giving us some concrete feedback to consider. What do the people who listen to us think about the way we preach? How long we preach for? The range of texts and topics we preach on?

To think back to the earlier section on 'being preached to', if we are part of a preaching or ministry team we may find that this can act as a resource for peer feedback and evaluation of our preaching. I can imagine some teams where that might not work, however, and it might be useful to have someone come in from outside to offer feedback and consultation. It's a simple idea, but it could be very influential. It would also be a fairly radical step, since many preachers work for decades without getting any structured or intentional feedback on their preaching. It may be something that individual presbyteries, dioceses or circuits should consider offering, perhaps creating

---

1 Examples can be found from British Methodists at: www.methodist.org. uk/media/560609/feedback_form_-_preaching_at_church.pdf, and from the Christian Reformed Church in the USA at http://cep.calvinseminary.edu/wp-content/uploads/2015/01/sermonEvaluationForm.pdf.

a few teams of 'constructive listeners' who could come to hear preachers and then meet to offer them confidential and constructive feedback?

I write as someone based in the Church of Scotland and two things are clearly true of our situation as a Church. The first is that preaching continues to be a central practice in the main Sunday act of Presbyterian worship in almost every congregation in our Church. The second is that most of our congregations are in long-term, sustained and significant decline. It is undoubtedly true that there are faithful churches that are not 'successful', and 'successful' churches that are not faithful, but when churches are declining they are wise to reflect on their own practice and how it might be shaped in the future.

We might think that this 'missional' dimension to evaluating preaching should try to find ways to listen to those who are dechurched, or unchurched, including ways to ask whether preaching is a practice that alienates people from church. We might also want to listen carefully to those within our denominations who are pioneers and church planters, and those who work with unchurched groups. Is preaching a problem? Are some kinds of preaching a problem? Are there examples of preachers changing their practice that the wider Church might want to learn from?

James 1:19 encourages us to be 'quick to listen, slow to speak, slow to anger'. I realise as I write this, that it is a text I have never preached on. But then, maybe in this context at least, that makes the point? There is a time to listen.

# Conclusion

Having written a good deal about form and genre, I am not completely sure what genre this book has been written in. It is a book on preaching written by an academic and it assumes readers who have had some academic training in theology and ministry. It is a wee book on homiletics, not a big one, and I offer it tentatively to more seasoned scholars of preaching, aware that it is a voice from the edges of their academic discipline. It is a work of practical theology, specifically of theological reflection on practice – both my own as a minister and teacher, and that of the wider Church, in so far as I know it. It is a book for the Church as well as the academy, and I hope that it will be of some use to ministers, pastors and those studying to be ordained or commissioned to the ministry of word and sacrament.

I always feel that those who write on preaching should let their readers see something of how they themselves preach, and since my sermons are not widely available online, I have included three of them here.

In contemporary Scottish and British culture, the idea of 'preaching' or being 'preachy' does not travel well beyond the Church. I am heartened, therefore, when I see African-American friends on social media in 2017 using the single word 'Preach!' to signal affirmation, encouragement and agreement. I like that it can still mean that, for some people at least. I have tried to write honestly about preaching and that has mostly been easy, because I still find preaching daunting. One of my own favourite books on preaching, *Countdown to Sunday* by Chris Erdman, is written 'for those who dare to preach', which is an apt phrase. Preaching is by no means the only work of the Church, but I still believe it is work that we in the Church are called to do and blessed in doing. So I end this book in solidarity with those of you who dare to preach and are daunted by what the Spirit dares you to do; in solidarity and in prayer for you: *God be in your mouths and in your speaking.*

# References and Bibliography

Baker, J. and Gay, D. 2003, *Alternative Worship*, London: SPCK.
Barth, K., 1928, 'The Need and Promise of Christian Preaching', in *The Word of God and the Word of Man*, London: Hodder & Stoughton.
Barth, K., 1975, *Church Dogmatics*, 1.1§4, p. 88.
Bethge, E., 1999, *Dietrich Bonhoeffer: A Biography*, Minneapolis, MI: Augsburg Fortress.
Bosch, D., 1991, *Transforming Mission*, Maryknoll, NY: Orbis.
Bourdieu, P., 1992, *The Logic of Practice*, Cambridge: Polity Press.
Bowen, R., ed., 2005, *A Guide to Preaching*, London: SPCK.
Bryan, C. and Landon, D., 2013, *Listening to the Bible: The Art of Faithful Biblical Interpretation*, Oxford: Oxford University Press.
Carroll, R., 1991, *Wolf in the Sheepfold – The Bible as a Problem for Christianity*, London: SPCK.
Currie, T. C., 2013, 'The Threefold Word of God in the Theology of Karl Barth', Edinburgh PhD thesis.
Dillard, Annie, 1982, *Teaching a Stone to Talk: Expeditions and Encounters*, New York: Harper & Row.
Erdman, C., 2007, *Countdown to Sunday*, Grand Rapids, MI: Brazos Press.
Fant, C., 1975, *Bonhoeffer's Preaching*, Nashville, TN: Thomas Nelson.
Forrester, D. and Gay, D., 2009, *Worship and Liturgy In Context*, London: SCM Press.
Freire, P., 1972, *The Pedagogy of the Oppressed*, Harmondsworth: Penguin.
Gay, D., 2011, *Remixing the Church*, London: SCM.
Gay, D., 2017, *Reforming the Kirk*, Edinburgh: St Andrew Press.
Gerrish, B., 1993, *Grace and Gratitude: The Eucharistic Theology of John Calvin*, Minneapolis, MI: Fortress Press.
Goldingay, J., 1993, 'How Far Do Reader's Make Sense?', Themelios, 18.2, January.
Hauerwas, S., 1974, *Vision and Virtue: Essays in Christian Ethical Reflection*, Notre Dame, IN: Fides/Claretian.
Jacks, G. Robert, 1981, *Just Say the Word – Writing for the Ear*, Grand Rapids, MI: Eerdmans.

Jeanrond, W., 1994, *Theological Hermeneutics*, London: SCM Press.

Kidner, D., 1983, *Preaching the Old Testament*, Edinburgh: Rutherford House.

Küng, H., 1977, *On Being a Christian*, London: William Collins.

Levinas, E., 1985, *Ethics and Infinity*, Pittsburgh, PA: Duquesne University Press.

Lewis, C. S., 1942, *The Screwtape Letters*, London: Centenary Press.

Loades, A., ed., 1990, *Feminist Theology: A Reader*, London: SPCK/ WJKP.

Long, T. G., 1989, *Preaching and the Literary Forms of the Bible*, Minneapolis, MI: Fortress Press.

Macintyre, A., 1981, *After Virtue*, London: Duckworth.

McCormack, B., 1997, *Karl Barth's Critically Realistic Dialectical Theology: Its Genesis and Development 1909–36*, New York: Oxford University Press, pp. 340–1.

McLellan, A., 1996, *Preaching for These People*, London: Mowbrays.

Moltmann, J., 1974, *The Crucified God*, London: SCM Press.

Moore, S. D., 1989, *Literary Criticism and the Gospels*, New Haven: Yale University Press.

Morley, J., 2004, *Bread of Tomorrow*, London: SPCK.

Newbigin, L., 1953/1964, *The Household of God*, London: SCM Press.

Newbigin, L., 1989, *The Gospel in a Pluralist Society*, London: SPCK.

Packer, J. I., 1993, *Knowing God*, London: Hodder & Stoughton.

Phillips, J. B., 1952, Introduction, *Letters to Young Churches*, London: Geoffrey Bles.

Parker, T. H. L., 1992, *Calvin's Preaching* (CO 26.67), Louisville, KY: Westminster John Knox Press.

Plantinga, Pauw, A., 2015, *Proverbs and Ecclesiastes*, Louisville, KY: Westminster John Knox Press.

Reddie, A. G., 2009, *Is God Colour Blind?* London: SPCK.

Ricoeur, P., 1970, *Freud and Philosophy: An Essay on Interpretations*, New Haven, CT, and London: Yale University Press.

Rienstra, R. and D. 2009, *Worship Words*, Grand Rapids, MI: Baker Academic.

Rose, Lucy Atkinson, 1997, *Sharing the Word – Preaching in the Roundtable Church*, Louisville, KY: Westminster John Knox Press.

Rudy-Froese, A., 2009, 'The Preached Sermon as a Happening of the Gospel', *Vision: A Journal for Church and Theology*, Spring.

Salley, Columbus and Behm, Ronald, 1973, *Your God Is Too White*, Tring: Lion Books.

Sanneh, L. 1989, *Translating the Message*, Maryknoll, NJ: Orbis.

Sell, Alan P., 2003, 'The Worship of English Congregationalism', in Vischer, L., ed., *Christian Worship in Reformed Churches Past and Present*, Grand Rapids, MI: Eerdmans, pp. 83–106.

Smith, J. K. A., 2006, *Who's Afraid of Postmodernism? Taking Derrida, Lyotard and Foucault to Church*, Grand Rapids, MI: Baker Academic.

Smith J. K. A., 2012, *The Fall of Interpretation* (4th edn), Grand Rapids, MI: Baker Academic.

Spinks, Bryan D., 2003, 'The Origins of the Antipathy to Set Liturgical Forms in the English-Speaking Reformed Tradition', in Vischer, L., ed., *Christian Worship in Reformed Churches Past and Present*, Grand Rapids, MI: Eerdmans, pp. 66–84.

Still, W., 1996, *The Work of the Pastor*, Carlisle: Rutherford House/Paternoster.

Stott, R., 2017, *In the Days of Rain*, London: Fourth Estate.

Stroupe, N. and Fleming, I., 1995, *While We Run This Race*, Maryknoll, NY: Orbis.

Vanhoozer, K. J., 1994, Finlayson Lecture, 'From Canon to Concept: "Same" and "Other" in the Relation between Biblical and Systematic Theology', *Journal of the Scottish Evangelical Theology Society*, 12.2 (Autumn), pp. 96–124.

Von Allmen, 1965, *Worship: Its Theology and Practice*, Oxford: Oxford University Press.

Wallis, J., 1981, *The Call to Conversion*, New York, NY: Harper Collins.

Walton, H. and Durber, S., 1994, *Silence in Heaven – A Book of Women's Preaching*, London: SCM.

Walton, H., 2014, *Writing Methods in Theological Reflection*, London: SCM Press.

Wells, S., 2001, *Be Not Afraid*, Grand Rapids, MI: Brazos Press.

Wells, S., 2002, 'How Common Worship Forms Local Character', *Studies in Christian Ethics* 15.1 pp. 66–74.

Wesley Allen Jr, O., ed., 2010, *The Renewed Homiletic*, Minneapolis, MN: Fortress Press.

Williams, Rowan, 1999, 'The Judgment of the World', in Williams, R., *On Christian Theology*, Oxford: Wiley Blackwell.

Wilson, P. S., 2008, Setting Words on Fire: Putting God at the Center of the Sermon, Nashville, TN: Abingdon Press.

Yancey, P., 1997, *What's So Amazing About Grace?*, Grand Rapids, MI: Zondervan.